✺ RAND McNALLY

W9-DFL-852

the road
atlas

MIDSIZE

CONTENTS

Travel Information

Best of the Road®

Each year our editors drive five new road trips to share with you those special things we call *Best of the Road*.

CENTER STAGE

Winnipeg, Manitoba, to Bismarck, North Dakota

The prairie is deceiving: what at first appears to be a wide expanse of flat nothing reveals itself, with a closer look, to be a teeming ecological system full of beautiful scenery, interesting stops, and tasty cuisine. All of that is enjoyed here via a look at North America's First Peoples and the settlers who came later, a jaunt through Canada's Manitoba province, and a hop across the border and into North Dakota. This journey takes in Manitoba's capital and largest city, Winnipeg, explores Riding Mountain National Park's vast wilderness, and looks at the bi-national International Peace Garden before ending with another capital, Bismarck.

Best known: Manitoba Museum and the Royal Winnipeg Ballet in Winnipeg; North Dakota State Capitol in Bismarck.

EDITOR'S PICKS

Manitoba Children's Museum (Winnipeg, MB)

Kids have too much fun to realize they're learning, while parents are happy to have the younger set along as an excuse to enjoy the vintage diesel locomotive, working TV studio, and various other exhibits and educational diversions at Winnipeg's Manitoba Children's Museum. *Kinsmen Building, 45 Forks Market Rd., (204) 924-4000, www.childrensmuseum.com*

Five Nations Gallery & Gifts (Mandan, ND)

Housed in a former railroad depot, the Five Nations retail arm of the Fort Abraham Lincoln Foundation provides a place for artists and musicians to sell a wide variety of CDs, paintings, beadwork, footwear, and more. *401 West Main St., (701) 663-4663, www.fortlincoln.com/five_nations_art.aspx*

More Great Stops

Mondragon Bookstore and Coffee House
91 Albert St.
Winnipeg, MB
(204) 946-5241
www.mondragon.ca

Le Musée de Saint-Boniface Museum
494 Tache Ave.
Saint-Boniface, MB
(204) 237-4500
www.msbm.mb.ca

FortWhyte Alive
1961 McCreary Rd.
Winnipeg, MB
(204) 989-8364
www.fortwhyte.org

MORE pictures, **MORE** attractions, **MORE** at go.randmcnally.com/br

North Dakota Heritage Center (Bismarck, ND)

An array of exhibits presents the North Dakota story at the Heritage Center, part of the state capitol complex, from the fossils of prehistoric beasts to the implements and artifacts of the humans who arrived and settled long after. *612 East Boulevard Ave., (701) 328-2666, www.nd.gov/hist/hcenter.htm*

Mariaggi's Theme Suite Hotel (Winnipeg, MB)

Travelers in the know use this kitschy-hip, surprisingly posh spot and its internationally themed rooms as home base for adventures in the surrounding counter-culture of the Exchange District. *231 McDermot Ave., (204) 947-9447, www.mariaggis.com*

EDITOR'S PICKS

Riding Mountain National Park (Wasagaming, MB)

Riding Mountain provides a natural nirvana for hikers, bikers, geocachers, snowshoers, bird watchers, and skiers, with almost 1,200 square miles of protected wilderness to explore and a wide variety of wildlife to see. *(204) 848-7275, www.pc.gc.ca/ridingmountain*

International Peace Garden (Dunseith, ND)

Begun as a 2,300-acre border-straddling statement about U.S.-Canadian friendship, the garden now includes a 9-11 Memorial, comprised of twisted girders from New York's World Trade Center. Visitors also take in a wildlife museum, café, gift shop, 1.5-mile hiking trail, and interpretive center. *10939 Highway 281, (701) 263-4390, www.peacegarden.com*

The Current Restaurant and Lounge

75 Forks Market Rd.
Winnipeg, MB
(204) 942-6555
www.innforks.com/dining/

Ft. Abraham Lincoln State Park

4480 Fort Lincoln Rd.
Mandan, ND
(701) 667-6380
www.fortlincoln.com

THE LASTING LANDSCAPE

Truth or Consequences to Las Cruces, New Mexico

This enchanting land reminds all who traverse here that the Old West is alive. It's a place where frontier is not a historical term. A trip through the serene wilderness of southwestern New Mexico starts in the quirky town of Truth or Consequences, winds and twists westward through the mountains to Silver City, then loops south and east to Deming and Las Cruces. By the time this rustic journey concludes, visitors to the Land of Enchantment return to civilization with a renewed sense of country, culture, and self.

Blackstone Hotsprings (Truth or Consequences)

Blackstone Hotsprings lures travelers with more than just 104-degree natural mineral water streaming directly into private, oversized tubs. Guests can stay in TV-show-inspired theme rooms, such as the Roy Rogers Suite and The Jetsons.
410 Austin St., (575) 894-0894, www.blackstonehotsprings.com

EDITOR'S PICKS

Palma's Italian Grill (Deming)

Palma's Italian Grill is a popular dining spot both for the building's historical significance and for the friendly service. Made-from-scratch menu favorites include lasagna, manicotti, and southwestern chicken pasta (with green chiles mixed into the alfredo sauce).
110 S. Silver Ave., (575) 544-3100

Best known: Elephant Butte Lake State Park; New Mexico State University in Las Cruces; Spaceport America* in Sierra County.

At press time, Spaceport America was scheduled to open in early 2010, and hundreds of tickets had already been sold for Virgin Galactic commercial space tourism flights. Keep up with the progress at www.spaceportamerica.com.

More Great Stops

Little Sprout Market and Juice Bar
400 N. Broadway St.
Truth or Consequences, NM
(575) 894-4114

Palace Hotel
106 W. Broadway St.
Silver City, NM
(575) 388-1811
www.zianet.com/palacehotel

Deming Luna Mimbres Museum and Custom House
310 S. Silver Ave.
Deming, NM
(575) 546-2382
www.deminglunamimbresmuseum.com/

Silver City Museum (Silver City)

The Silver City Museum serves as the "Treasure Vault of New Mexico," with more than 20,000 artifacts in its collection. A third-floor cupola overlooks the hill where silver was originally discovered and where the Legal Tender mine was located in 1870. *312 W. Broadway St., (575) 538-5921, www.silvercitymuseum.org*

Nambé (Old Mesilla)

New Mexico treasure Nambé is beautiful and useful: it retains hot or cold temperatures and resembles silver but does not chip or tarnish. The Nambé store on the Old Mesilla square offers the complete line of products, including the eight-metal Nambé Alloy. *2109 Calle de Parian, (575) 527-4623, www.nambe.com*

EDITOR'S PICKS

Chile Pepper Institute (Las Cruces)

The Chile Pepper Institute enlightens visitors about the "hottest" crop around. The institute sells seeds for growing chile peppers and cookbooks for preparing them, and provides guided tours of a colorful chile garden filled with more than 200 types of chile pepper. *College St. and Knox St. MSC 3Q, New Mexico State University, (575) 646-3028, www.chilepepperinstitute.org*

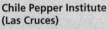
New Mexico Farm & Ranch Museum

4100 Dripping Springs Rd.
Las Cruces, NM
(575) 522-4100
www.nmfarmandranchmuseum.org

La Posta de Mesilla

2410 Calle de San Albino
Mesilla, NM
(575) 524-3524
www.laposta-de-mesilla.com

EDITOR'S PICKS

Corning Museum of Glass (Corning)

Inside a landmark glass building, the Corning Museum of Glass demonstrates glassblowing and glass breaking. Visitors can make their own glass objects ($10-$27) or purchase an heirloom at the GlassMarket. *One Museum Way, (800) 732-6845, www.cmog.org*

New York Wine & Culinary Center (Canandaigua)

At the New York Wine & Culinary Center, the LeCesse Garden shows off New York State crops, while the hands-on kitchen offers cooking classes. Meals at the Taste of New York Lounge feature New York ingredients and are paired with local beers and wine. *800 South Main St., (585) 394-7070, www.nywcc.com*

CULTIVATING NEW YORK

Canandaigua to Cooperstown, New York

There's no straight shot through upstate New York, not with those lakes in the way. But with all the good food to sample, it's worth taking the drive easy along the Finger Lakes, over the hills, through the farmland, and into river valleys. This road trip begins in Canandaigua, at the northern end of a western Finger Lake, and meanders south to Corning, then north to Ithaca, and gradually east toward Herkimer until it ends near the other great New York waterway, the Mohawk River Valley. New Yorkers and visitors are renewing attention to the land: the food grown here, the ecology that sustains farms and wildlife populations, and the waterways that fostered and transported culture across the state.

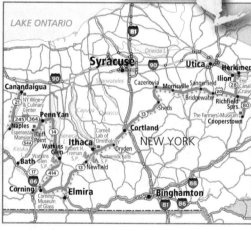

Best known: Watkins Glen International Raceway; Glenora Wine Cellars in Dundee; Baseball Hall of Fame in Cooperstown.

More Great Stops

Bully Hill Vineyards
8843 Greyton H. Taylor Memorial Drive
Hammondsport, NY
(607) 868-3210
www.bullyhill.com

Seward House
33 South St.
Auburn, NY
(315) 252-1283
www.sewardhouse.org

Oneida Community Mansion House
170 Kenwood Ave.
Oneida, NY
(315) 363-0745
www.oneidacommunity.org

MORE pictures, MORE attractions, MORE at go.randmcnally.com/br

The Farmers' Museum (Cooperstown)

At The Farmers' Museum, costumed interpreters carry out daily tasks in many of the 26 historic buildings. Twenty-four hand-carved animals carry children around the Empire State Carousel while parents read about famous New Yorkers on the carousel's frieze. *5775 NY 80, (888) 547-1450, www.farmersmuseum.org*

Cornell Lab of Ornithology (Ithaca)

At the Cornell Lab of Ornithology Visitors' Center, sample birdsong and make your own in the replica sound studio, try out powerful scopes, and stock up on birding equipment. Four-and-a-half miles of easy trails wind through 220-acre Sapsucker Woods. *159 Sapsucker Woods Rd., (800) 843-2473, www.birds.cornell.edu*

EDITOR'S PICKS

Erie Canal Cruise (Herkimer)

For 90 minutes aboard the *Lil' Diamond II* cruise boat, Captain Jerry entertains with tales of the Erie Barge Canal. When the Lock 18 doors close, the lock house seems to rise into the air as slimy walls creep up alongside the boat. *800 Mohawk St., (315) 715-0350, www.eriecanalcruises.com*

Esperanza Mansion (Bluff Point)

Esperanza Mansion overlooks Keuka Lake; its kitchen offers meals inside the Greek Revival house, outside on the patio, or aboard the *Esperanza Rose* tour boat. Puff pastry enfolds the warm turkey and brie sandwich, a local favorite ($14). *3456 NY 54A, (866) 927-4400, www.esperanzamansion.com*

Erie Canal Village
5789 Rome New London Rd.
 (NY 46/49)
Rome, NY
(315) 337-3999
www.eriecanalvillage.net

Fly Creek Cider Mill and Orchard
288 Goose St.
Fly Creek, NY
(800) 505-6455
www.flycreekcidermill.com

EDITOR'S PICKS

Upper Klamath National Wildlife Refuge canoe trail (Rocky Point, OR)

Rent a canoe (at The Ledge in Klamath Falls or from Rocky Point Resort) or bring your own craft for a paddle along a waterway trail where wildlife abounds. Look for osprey, white pelicans, even eagles fishing. *Rocky Point Resort, 28121 Rocky Point Rd., (530) 667-2230, www.fws.gov/klamathbasinrefuges/*

Nibbley's Cafe (Klamath Falls, OR)

Oatcakes, a substantial pancake that can be topped with blueberries, pecans, or bananas, are the house specialty for breakfast at this friendly local hangout. Lunch staples include fresh oat bread sandwiches and wraps. *2650 Washburn Way, Ste. 120, (541) 883-2314*

VOLCANIC LEGACY

Crater Lake, Oregon, to Mt. Shasta, California

Poor Lewis and Clark. They culminated their 1804 cross-country trek in a miserable nonstop rainy season at Ft. Clatsop, in the far northwestern corner of Oregon. If they'd only come down to south-central Oregon, starting just past present-day Eugene, they would have found abundant wildlife and rivers, spied the beautiful blue of Crater Lake, seen amazing formations in Oregon Caves just west of today's Medford. Further south, in California, they would have walked the eerie landscape that is now Lava Beds National Monument and hiked the majestic Shasta Cascade Mountains. Today's visitor can circle back up into Oregon for stops at wineries, cheese factories, and boutique chocolate producers along with gourmet restaurants in the Medford/Ashland area. Adventurous types go for the river rafting and jetboating (in Grants Pass), kayaking and canoeing wilderness trails, bicycling rail trails, a treehouse resort or even a railroad car motel. It's truly an explorer's paradise.

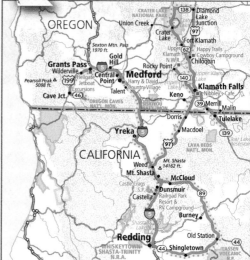

Best known: Crater Lake; Lava Beds National Park; Mt. Shasta; Ashland Shakespeare Festival in Ashland.

More Great Stops

Hi-Lo Cafe
88 S. Weed Blvd.
Weed, CA
(530) 938-2904
www.sisdevco.com/cafe.html

Sundial Bridge at Turtle Bay
1335 Arboretum Drive
Redding, CA
(530) 242-3143
www.turtlebay.org

Oregon Caves National Monument Big Tree Loop Trail
19000 Caves Hwy.
Cave Junction, OR
(541) 592-2100
www.nps.gov/orca

MORE pictures, MORE attractions, MORE at go.randmcnally.com/br

Railroad Park Resort and RV Campground (Dunsmuir, CA)

Spend the night in your own caboose or rail car, all outfitted as motel rooms. The Shasta Cascades serve as a gorgeous natural backdrop for the resort. The RV Campground features an old-time popular "swimming hole" and sandy beach. *100 Railroad Park Rd., (530) 235-4440, www.rrpark.com*

Harry & David Country Village (Medford, OR)

Tour the famed and extensive catalog operations, past rows of chocolate dippers and fruit and basket packers, then use the $5 tour fee toward purchasing fresh pears or other food goodies at the store afterward. *1314 Center Dr., (877) 322-8000, www.harryanddavid.com*

EDITOR'S PICKS

Happy Trails Cowboy Campground (Chiloquin, OR)

Sign up for a custom trail ride into Winema National Forest, enjoy a cowboy steak dinner by the campfire, and sleep in a platform tent or in your own RV at this horse-friendly campground that also welcomes your family pet. *46925 Hwy. 97 North, (541) 783-3559, www.happytrailscowboycampground.com*

Hellgate Jetboat Excursions (Grants Pass, OR)

Ride the wild Rogue River at breakneck speeds in a jetboat. The pace slows only to check out osprey nests, beaver dams, and other wildlife. Excursions range from two-hour blasts to five-hour power rides ($37 to $62 for adults). *966 SW 6th St., (800) 648-4874, www.hellgate.com*

■ **Rogue Creamery Store**
311 N. Front St.
Central Point, OR
(541) 665-1155
www.roguecreamery.com

■ **Dragonfly Café and Gardens**
241 Hargadine St.
Ashland, OR
(541) 488-4855
www.dragonflyashland.com

MORE pictures, MORE attractions, MORE at go.randmcnally.com/br

Kudzu Kabin Designs (Walhalla)

Native American and local fiber artist Nancy Basket finds practical use for each part of the Japanese-import kudzu plant. Visitors can create their own baskets, learn the paper-making process, and choose from dozens of prints, art cards, baskets, soaps, and jellies in her shop. *1105 E. Main St., (864) 718-8864, www.nancybasket.com*

EDITOR'S PICKS

Old Town Bistro (Rock Hill)

The Old Town Bistro honors the 1961 Friendship Nine civil rights protest with the original barstools at the counter. Patrons learn about the event through photos and a historical marker, then enjoy Southern-style classics such as broasted chicken with fried okra and fried squash. *135 E. Main St., (803) 327-9222, www.rholdtownbistro.com*

SOUTHERN CHARM

Rock Hill to Greenwood, South Carolina

Tucked neatly between the Appalachian Mountains and the Atlantic Ocean is humble Upcountry South Carolina. Revolutionary War and Civil War battlefields engage generations of history enthusiasts, while forests, rivers, and steep waterfalls create a natural playground. Beginning in Rock Hill, this drive along rolling country roads heads north to follow the Cherokee Foothills National Scenic Highway (SC 11), then continues south to Abbeville and Greenwood.

The scenery and adventure opportunities abound amid the Deep South's truest charms: history and hospitality.

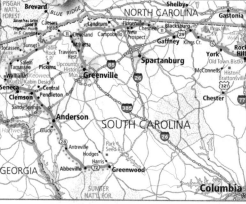

Best known: Carowinds amusement park in Charlotte; Chattooga River (film site for *Deliverance*); Cowpens National Battlefield in Gaffney; Clemson University in Clemson.

More Great Stops

■ **Sanders Farm Stand**
2275 Filbert Hwy.
Filbert, SC
(803) 684-9156
www.dorisanders.com

■ **Carolina Foothills Artisan Center**
124 W. Cherokee St.
Chesnee, SC
(864) 461-3050
www.cfac.us

■ **Hagood Mill**
307 Johnson St.
Pickens, SC
(864) 898-2936
www.co.pickens.sc.us/culturalcommission/

Historic Brattonsville (McConnells)
Costumed interpreters enlighten visitors about Historic Brattonsville's role in history, especially the Revolutionary War and slavery. An eight-and-a-half-mile network of hiking/mountain bike trails includes a battlefield trail and a nature trail.
1444 Brattonsville Rd., (803) 684-2327, www.chmuseums.org

Park Seed Co. (Hodges)
A tour of the Park Seed Co.'s headquarters reveals a horticulture wonderland, with more than 48,000 flowers, vegetables, shrubs, and trees. The on-site Garden Center sells seeds, unusual plants and bulbs, and unique and useful gardening accessories.
3507 Cokesbury Rd., (864) 223-8555, www.parkseed.com

Upcountry History Museum (Greenville)
Upcountry history comes to life via multimedia and sound and light presentations, covering everything from wars and textiles to Shoeless Joe Jackson. Children enjoy having their picture taken with the iconic pigs in the lobby, then taking a souvenir pig mascot home ($5).
540 Buncombe St., (864) 467-3100, www.upcountryhistory.org

EDITOR'S PICKS

Table Rock State Park (Pickens)
In the deep, densely forested foothills of the Blue Ridge Mountains, visitors to Table Rock State Park enjoy swimming, canoeing and paddle boating, fishing, and hiking a variety of trails, including to the top of Table Rock Mountain.
158 E. Ellison Ln., (864) 878-9813, www.southcarolinaparks.com

Split Creek Farm
3806 Centerville Rd.
Anderson, SC
(864) 287-3921
www.splitcreek.com

Hearthside Manor
1304 N. Main St.
Abbeville, SC
(864) 366-6555
www.hearthsidemanorbedandbreakfast.com

ROAD WORK

Road construction and road conditions resources

Road closed. Single lane traffic ahead. Detour.

When you are on the road, knowledge is power. Let Rand McNally help you avoid situations that can result in delays, or worse.

There are ways to prepare for construction traffic and avoid the dangers of poor road conditions. Read on:

1. Use the state and province websites and hotlines listed on this page for road construction and road conditions information.

2. Visit go.randmcnally.com/roadconstruction for current U.S. and Canadian road construction information.

Get the Info from the 511 hotline

The U.S. Federal Highway Administration has begun implementing a national system of highway and road conditions/construction information for travelers. Under the new plan, travelers can dial 511 and get up-to-date information on roads and highways.

Implementation of 511 is the responsibility of state and local agencies.

For more details, visit:
www.fhwa.dot.gov/trafficinfo/511.htm.

Get updated road construction info and get rolling.

Register your 2010 Rand McNally Road Atlas and get FREE access to premium road construction information.

- Road construction maps
- Detailed, accurate information
- Project dates
- Trip-specific information

go.randmcnally.com/roadatlas

- ▣ Road conditions
- ⚒ Road construction
- ● Both

United States

Alabama
www.dot.state.al.us/docs ●

Alaska
511 ●
(866) 282-7577 ●
511.alaska.gov ●
In AK: (800) 478-7675 ▣

Arizona
511 ●
(888) 411-7623 ●
www.az511.com ●

Arkansas
(800) 245-1672 ▣
(501) 569-2000 ▣
(501) 569-2227 ●
www.arkansashighways.com ●

California
(916) 445-7623 ⚒
www.dot.ca.gov
San Francisco Bay area: 511 ●,
www.511.org ●
Sacramento Region: 511 ●,
www.sacregion511.org ●
San Diego: 511,
www.511sd.com ●
In CA: (800) 427-7623 ▣

Colorado
511 ●
(303) 639-1111 ●
www.cotrip.org ●
In CO: (877) 315-7623 ●

Connecticut
(860) 594-2000 ▣
www.ct.gov/dot ●
In CT: (800) 443-6817 ●

Delaware
www.deldot.net ●
In DE: (800) 652-5600 ●
Out of state: (302) 760-2080 ●

Florida
511 ●
www.fl511.com ●
www.dot.state.fl.us ●

Georgia
511 ●
(877) 694-2511 ●
(404) 635-8000 ●
www.511ga.org ●
www.georgia-navigator.com ●

Hawaii
(808) 536-6566 ⚒
www.hawaii.gov/dot/highways/
roadwork/ ⚒

Idaho
511 ●
(888) 432-7623 ●
511.idaho.gov ●

Illinois
(800) 452-4368 ●
www.gettingaroundillinois.com ●

Indiana
(800) 261-7623 ▣
(317) 232-5533 ▣
www.in.gov/dot ●

Iowa
511 ●
(800) 288-1047 ●
www.511ia.org ●

Kansas
511 ●
(800) 585-7623 ●
511.ksdot.org ●

Kentucky
511 ●
(866) 737-3767 ●
www.511.ky.gov ●

Louisiana
(888) 762-3511 ●
www.511la.org ●

Maine
511 ●
(866) 282-7578 ●
(207) 624-3595 ●
www.511maine.gov ●

Maryland
(800) 543-2515 ●
(410) 582-5650 ●
www.chart.state.md.us ●

Massachusetts
511 ●
(617) 374-1234 ●
www.mhd.state.ma.us/ ●

Michigan
(800) 381-8477 ●
www.michigan.gov/mdot/ ●
Metro Detroit: (800) 641-6368 ▲

Minnesota
511 ●
(800) 657-3774 ●
(651) 296-3000 ●
www.511mn.org ●

Mississippi
(601) 359-7017 ●
www.mstraffic.com ●

Missouri
(800) 222-6400 ▲
(888) 275-6636 ●
(573) 751-2551 ●
St. Louis Gateway: 511 ●,
(877) 478-5511 ●,
www.gatewayguide.com/atis/
index.html ●
www.modot.mo.gov ●

Montana
511 ●
(800) 226-7623 ●
www.mdt.mt.gov/travinfo/511 ●

Nebraska
511 ●
(800) 906-9069 ●
(402) 471-4533 ●
www.nebraskatransportation.
org ●

Nevada
511 ●
(877) 687-6237 ●
www.safetravelusa.com/nv/ ●

New Hampshire
511 ●
(866) 282-7579 ●
www.nh.gov/dot/511 ●

New Jersey
511 ●
www.state.nj.us/transportation/
commuter/511/conditions.shtm ●
Turnpike: (800) 336-5875 ●,
www.state.nj.us/turnpike/ ●
Garden State Parkway:
(732) 727-5929 ●,
www.state.nj.us/turnpike/gsp-
conditions.htm ●

New Mexico
(800) 432-4269 ●
www.nmroads.com ●

New York
www.nysdot.gov ●
(518) 457-6195
Thruway: (800) 847-8929 ●,
www.thruway.state.ny.us ●

North Carolina
511 ●
(877) 511-4662 ●
www.ncdot.org/traffictravel ●

North Dakota
511 ●
(866) 696-3511 ●
www.dot.nd.gov/divisions/
maintenance/511_nd.html ●

Ohio
(614) 644-7031 ▲
www.buckeyetraffic.org ●
Cincinnati/northern Kentucky
area: 511 ●, (513) 333-3333 ●,
www.artimis.org ●
Turnpike: (440) 234-2030 ▲,
(888) 876-7453 ●,
www.ohioturnpike.org ●
In OH: (888) 264-7623 ●

Oklahoma
(888) 425-2385 ▲
(405) 425-2385 ▲
www.okladot.state.ok.us ●

Oregon
511 ●
(800) 977-6368 ●
(503) 588-2941 ●
www.tripcheck.com ●

Pennsylvania
(717) 783-5186 ●
www.dot7.state.pa.us/
TravelerInformation/ ●
In PA: (888) 783-6783 ●

Rhode Island
511 ●
Outside RI: (888) 401-4511 ●
www2.tmc.state.ri.us ●

South Carolina
www.dot.state.sc.us ●

South Dakota
511 ●
(866) 697-3511 ●
www.sddot.com/travinfo.asp ●

Tennessee
511 ●
(877) 244-0065 ●
www.tn511.com ●

Texas
(800) 452-9292 ●
www.dot.state.tx.us/travel/ ●

Utah
511 ●
(800) 492-2400 ●
(866) 511-8824 ●
www.utahcommuterlink.com ●

Vermont
511 ●
(800) 429-7623 ●
www.aot.state.vt.us/
travelinfo.htm ●
www.511vt.com ●

Virginia
511 ●
(800) 578-4111 ●
(800) 367-7623 ●
www.511virginia.org ●

Washington
511 ●
(800) 695-7623 ●
www.wsdot.wa.gov/traffic/ ●

Washington, D.C.
311 ●
(202) 727-1000 ●
www.ddot.dc.gov/ ●

West Virginia
(877) 982-7623 ▦
www.wvdot.com ●

Wisconsin
(800) 762-3947 ●
www.dot.state.wi.us/travel/
incident-alerts.htm ●

Wyoming
511 ▦
(888) 996-7623 ▦
www.dot.state.wy.us ●
www.wyoroad.info ●

Canada
Alberta
(403) 246-5853 ●
(877) 262-4997 ●
www.trans.gov.ab.ca ●
www.ama.ab.ca ●

British Columbia
(800) 550-4997 ●
www.drivebc.ca/ ●

Manitoba
(204) 945-3704 ●
www.gov.mb.ca/roadinfo/ ●
In MB: (877) 627-6237 ●

New Brunswick
www1.gnb.ca/cnb/
transportation/index-e.asp ●
In NB: (800) 561-4063 ▦

Newfoundland & Labrador
www.roads.gov.nl.ca ●

Nova Scotia
511 ●
(902) 424-3933 ▦
www.gov.ns.ca/tran ●
In NS: (800) 307-7669 ▦

Ontario
www.mto.gov.on.ca/english/
traveller/ ●
In ON: (800) 268-4686 ●
In Toronto: (416) 235-4686 ●

Prince Edward Island
(902) 368-4770 ●
(Nov–May 24 hours;
Jun-Oct daytime only)
www.gov.pe.ca/roadconditions ▦

Québec
(888) 355-0511 ●
www.inforoutiere.qc.ca ●
In Québec: (877) 393-2363 ●

Saskatchewan
(888) 335-7623 ●
www.highways.gov.sk.ca/
road-conditions ●

Mexico
www.sct.gob.mx ●
(in Spanish only)

EAT YOUR WAY ACROSS THE USA
and Canada too!

From gator bashes and annual spud days to the Great Wisconsin Cheese Festival, there are food hot spots all across the U.S.A. and Canada. Check out these 30 food festivals—plus a few suggestions for a side trip to savor a favorite local dish.

Hatch Valley Chile Festival

Swamp Cabbage Festival

February
La Belle, Florida

Don't let the name scare you—"swamp cabbage" is just the local term for heart of palm. Tender, ivory-colored, and tasting somewhat like artichoke, swamp cabbage is harvested from the stem, or "heart," of Florida's state tree, the sabal palm. La Belle's festival honoring this delicacy also features gospel music, armadillo races, a parade, rodeo, goods made by members of the Seminole tribe, and, of course, lots of swamp cabbage, served raw, stewed, or frittered. *(863) 675-2995, www.swampcabbagefestival.org*

National Date Festival

February
Indio, California

Sorry, lonely hearts, the date we're talking about here is the fibrous fruit, not the romantic rendezvous. Some 250,000 date palms sway over California's Coachella Valley, producing 35 million pounds of dates annually. Witness the ceremonial Blessing of the Dates, famous for camel and ostrich races, check out elaborate date exhibits, and sample more than 50 varieties of dates, including sweet medjools, delicate deglet noors, and caramel-like amer hajjs. *(760) 863-8247, www.datefest.org*

World Catfish Festival

April
Belzoni, Mississippi

With more than 30,000 acres of land under water and more catfish acreage than any other state, Humphreys County deserves the nickname "Catfish Capital of the World." What better place, then, for the world's largest catfish fry? Sample a genuine Southern midday dinner of fried catfish, hush puppies, and coleslaw. Or save your appetite for the catfish-eating contest: Entrants have 10 minutes to devour three pounds of hot catfish fillets. *(800) 408-4838, www.catfishcapitalonline.com*

LOCAL DISH DETOUR

To: Tampa, Florida
(150 miles NW of La Belle)

Trying to order Spanish bean soup in Spain will get you nowhere, even if you ask nicely ("Garbanzo sopa, por favor"). This dish, made with garbanzo beans, ham and beef bones, salt pork, chorizo, and potatoes, is more or less available only in Florida, specifically Tampa, where it was invented at the Columbia Restaurant (2117 East 7th Ave.) around 1910. Enjoy a bowl while taking in one of the $6 flamenco shows here. Other Tampa soup spots: Carmine's Restaurant & Bar (1802 E. 7th Ave.), which offers it with a half-sandwich on the side, and La Tropicana Café, just down the street (1822 E. 7th Ave.).

Stockton Asparagus Festival

April

Stockton, California

Stockton has asparagus to spare: tons are cooked during this weekend extravaganza. Fried asparagus is the most popular dish, but asparagus nachos, asparagus pasta, and asparagus margaritas are also on the menu. Watch the asparagus eating contest: contestants have 10 minutes to eat as many "green spears" as they can, then pose for pics with festival mascots Gus and Brit-Nee Spears.

(209) 644-3740, www.asparagusfest.com

Great Wisconsin Cheese Festival

June

Little Chute, Wisconsin

Cheeseheads of the world, this festival's for you. At the free cheese tasting, you can sample more than 30 types of cheese, including Wisconsin's native Colby. And no Dairy State experience would be complete without those peanut-sized munchies known as cheese curds. (Connoisseurs say they're best deep-fried.) Don't miss the cheese-carving demos, where barns, cows, and other sculptures take form out of behemoth blocks of cheddar. But please, don't eat the art! *(920) 788-7390, www.littlechutewi.org/calendar_events/cheesefest.html*

LOCAL DISH DETOUR

To: San Francisco, California (80 miles W of Stockton)

Cioppino (say chih-PEEN-oh), a fish and tomato stew, is said to have its origins in the early-1900s Italian fishing community of San Francisco. Try it at Cioppino's on Fisherman's Wharf (400 Jefferson St.), which serves it with grilled sourdough toast, or Scoma's (Pier 47 on Al Scoma Way), where you can have it with a half crab. At the Tadich Grill (240 California St.)—open since 1849—diners can order a bowl of the house cioppino while sitting in the semi-private booths.

LOCAL DISH DETOUR

To: Racine, Wisconsin (144 miles S of Little Chute)

It takes three days to make kringle, the oval coffee cake that Danish immigrants brought to Racine, Wisconsin in the 1800s, the traditional way. Fortunately, the town brims with bakeries that will do the work for you. The O&H Danish Bakery (1841 Douglas Ave. and 4006 Durand Ave.) is a kringle addict's delight—not only can you buy the pastry on site, you can also sign up for the Kringle-of-the-Month Club. Other pastry enablers: Larsen's Bakery (3311 Washington Ave.), and Lehmann's Bakery (4900 Spring St.), which offers a banana-split version by special order.

Vidalia Onion Festival

April

Vidalia, Georgia

If the thought of biting into an onion brings tears to your eyes, you haven't tried a Vidalia. Not just anyone can grow a Vidalia—the Georgia legislature restricts production of this mild, sweet onion to a 20-county growing area. Munching on raw onions is common practice at this festival, but those who prefer 'em deep-fried can nosh on "blooming onions" and onion rings. There's also an onion cook-off and an onion-eating contest. All events are BYOBM: Bring Your Own Breath Mints. *(912) 538-8687, www.vidaliaonionfestival.com*

Pink Tomato Festival

June

Warren, Arkansas

Bradley County's prize produce might look a little under-ripe, but this is one tomato that's supposed to be pink. Unfortunately, the fruit isn't usually shipped because it bruises easily, so southern Arkansas might be the only place to sample what local folks call "the world's tastiest tomato." Taste it for yourself at Warren's festival, which features a tomato-eating contest, pink salsa competition, and an all-tomato luncheon . . . tomato carrot cake, anyone?

(870) 226-5225, www.bradleypinktomato.com

This isn't just any old corn either—it's Olathe Sweet, and it's extra sweet.

International Horseradish Festival
June
Collinsville, Illinois

Not only is Collinsville home to the world's largest ketchup bottle, it's also the Horseradish Capital of the World! The bottomlands of the Mississippi are fertile ground for the zesty root, producing more than 60 percent of the world's horseradish each year. This annual celebration features a Root Toss, a recipe contest (mmm. . . horseradish apple pie!), and Root Golf, played with balls carved from horseradish. Pick up a jar of horseradish relish or horseradish jelly to kick your next meal up a notch. *(618) 344-2884, www.horseradishfestival.com*

Paella y Vino Festival
June
Tijuana, Mexico

Paella lovers will be in heaven. This open-air event brings out the best in the rice dish that originated in Valencia, Spain. Paella is the word for "frying pan," and creative cooks differ on what to put in the popular dish that is cooked in big shallow pans. Vegetables, seafood, and meat are the usual ingredients, but the annual paella competition features new recipes as well. Sip some Baja California wine, listen to Mexican music, watch folk dancers, and discover for yourself why paella is considered the food of kings. *(888) 775-2417, www.seetijuana.com*

Fish, Fun & Folk Festival
July
Twillingate, Newfoundland & Labrador

There are many reasons to visit the tranquil village of Twillingate: the spectacular coastline, the towering blue icebergs that drift down from the Arctic, the humpback whales just offshore, the friendly people, and of course the annual Fish, Fun & Folk Festival. This celebration of Newfoundland culture and heritage draws top folk musicians from throughout the province. When the fiddling stops, festivalgoers head to the dining hall for traditional Newfoundland meals of cod, salmon, and lobster. *(709) 884-2678, www.fishfunfolkfestival.com*

Olathe Sweet Corn Festival
August
Olathe, Colorado

Nothing says summer like fresh corn-on-the-cob, and in the tiny town of Olathe they've got plenty to give away on festival day (more than 70,000 free ears!). This isn't just any old corn either—it's Olathe Sweet, and it's extra sweet. This special strain grows best in the Uncompahgre Valley, where locals proclaim it "the best sweet corn on the planet." If you're an old pro at cleaning the cob, try chomping past the corn-eating contest record: 32 ears in 12 minutes. *(866) 363-2676, www.olathesweetcornfest.com*

Vermont State Zucchini Fest
August
Ludlow, Vermont

At festival time, Ludlow becomes a zucchini zoo. Kids zoom to the zucchini-carving and "Dress Your Zucchini Doll" contests, and green-thumbed locals produce their biggest produce for the squash weigh-in. At the "Taste of Zucchini," zuke zealots feast on dishes like zucchini-lemon sorbet and cold zucchini soup, while the less adventurous squash their appetites with fried zucchini and zucchini bread. So if you're zany for zucchini, Ludlow's the place to be in August. *(802) 228-5830, www.yourplaceinvermont.com*

Blackberry Festival

August

Powell River, British Columbia

Blackberry vines are as ubiquitous in coastal British Columbia as kudzu in Mississippi. Rubus armeniacus generally is considered a thorny nuisance, but the people of Powell River celebrate its plump, sweet fruit each summer with a street party, music, clowns, and, of course, lots of blackberries. Dessert contests for amateur and professional chefs yield delectable dishes like blackberry crème brûlée and blackberry dessert pizza. Winning chefs usually can be persuaded to share their recipes.
(604) 483-9454
www.discoverpowellriver.com/visitors/Blackberry.htm

LOCAL DISH DETOUR

To: Vancouver, British Columbia (108 miles SE of Powell River)

Wild salmon have inhabited the pristine Pacific Northwest waters for thousands of years. The five species of Pacific salmon are sold as delicacies in many international markets. The mighty chinook, or king salmon can grow up to 126 pounds and is a rare catch; the other four are coho, sockeye, pink, and chum. In downtown Vancouver, Salmon Village (779 Thurlow St.) sells a variety of salmon products, including sockeye and king smoked salmon, salmon candy (smoked salmon marinated in pure Canadian maple syrup), and salmon jerky.

National Lentil Festival

August

Pullman, Washington

Having trouble getting the kids to eat their lentils? Treat them to some of the leguminous delicacies at this festival, and they'll never know what hit 'em. In the past, lentil chocolate cake, lentil cookies, and lentil ice cream have topped the list of unusual creations offered in Pullman, heart of the largest U.S. lentil-producing region. Festival highlights include a parade led by mascot Tase T. Lentil, a lentil cook-off, and more than 200 gallons of free lentil chili.
(800) 365-6948, www.lentilfest.com

AppleJack Festival

September

Nebraska City, Nebraska

More than 36,000 bushels of apples are picked from orchards around Nebraska City, which celebrates with an apple-fest each September. Held at different locations around town, activities include picking your own apples at local orchards, craft vendors, and a parade. Try all sorts of apple-based goodies, including apple fritters, caramel apples, and apple cider. As part of the festival, the AppleJam Fest hosts family activities at the local school.
(800) 514-9113, www.nebraskacity.com/new/applejack08.html

Pick your own apples from Nebraska City's local orchards.

Hard Crab Derby and Fair
September

Crisfield, Maryland

Find a fast crab, because this event's all about pinching out the competition. About 350 of the clawed critters race down a wooden board, vying for trophies for their human cheerleaders. There's also a Governor's Cup race, in which crabs representing all 50 states try to out-scuttle each other. (Winners are spared the pot.) A crab-picking contest and a crab-cooking contest round out the festivities.
(800) 782-3913, www.crisfieldchamber.com/crabderby.htm

Hatch Valley Chile Festival
September

Hatch, New Mexico

The "Chile Capital of the World" celebrates the harvest with a Chile Queen pageant, a cooking demonstration where you can learn how to prepare the hot peppers for use in sauces and relishes, chile-eating contests, and a chile decorating contest. Jalapeños, nachos, serranos, and other varieties are served in enchiladas, empañadas,  burritos, chile relleños, and chile con carne. If you can take the heat, head to Hatch for this fiery festival. It might take a few days, but the burning in your mouth will eventually fade away.
(575) 267-5050, www.hatchchilefest.com

The Louisiana Shrimp & Petroleum Festival
September

Morgan City, Louisiana

Have no fear: Cajun Country's two most important resources are kept separate at all times at this festival. Feast on shrimp cooked in so many ways it would "make Forrest Gump proud," then take in the Blessing of the Fleet and the Water Parade, where decorated shrimp trawlers and oil boats motor up and down the Atchafalaya River. *(985) 385-0703, www.shrimp-petrofest.org*

LOCAL DISH DETOUR

To: New Orleans, Louisiana (85 miles NE of Morgan City)

Only two things interrupt business at New Orleans's 146-year-old Café du Monde—Christmas Day and hurricanes. Otherwise, both locals and tourists come to the café's original French Quarter location (800 Decatur St.) 24 hours a day, seven days a week for beignets, the fried squares of dough blanketed with powdered sugar and best consumed with a cup of chicory coffee or a steaming café au lait. Nearby at 819 Decatur St., Café Beignet has shorter hours but a more extensive menu. In addition to beignets, here you can try other Cajun specialties such as gumbo. (Both Café du Monde and Café Beignet have other locations around the city, too.) Before the Morning Call Coffee Stand moved outside the city to Metairie (two locations: 3325 Severn Ave. and 4436 Veterans Memorial Blvd. in the Clearview Mall), it too lay in the French Quarter, where it opened in 1870. But its Severn Avenue location still serves beignets around the clock. Wherever you go, be prepared for the unavoidable powdered sugar fallout on your clothes.

McClure Bean Soup Festival and Fair

September

McClure, Pennsylvania

At this festival, ground beef, beans, and lard slowly simmer in 35-gallon iron kettles just like they did back when the Blue fought the Gray. The festival began in 1891, when Civil War vets got together and cooked up their typical wartime fare at a public dinner. Today, descendants of those veterans and citizens of McClure stir the soup for more than 75,000 festival-goers. Fireworks, parades, and Civil War reenactments top off the annual celebration.

(800) 338-7389, www.mcclurebeansoup.com

Texas Gatorfest

September

Anahuac, Texas

Does alligator really taste like chicken? Find out at this three-day celebration in the Alligator Capital of Texas, where gators outnumber people three to one. Food booths offer such reptilian fare as alligator sausage, fried alligator, grilled alligator legs, and alligator jerky. The festival also features airboat rides, live music, vendors selling alligator products, beauty pageants, and the Great Texas Alligator Roundup, in which hunters compete to bring in the biggest gator. (The winners often exceed 13 feet!)

(409) 267-4190, www.texasgatorfest.com

LOCAL DISH DETOUR

To: Philadelphia, Pennsylvania (168 miles SE of McClure)

The proper components of a Philadelphia cheese steak are the subject of intense controversy. Is Cheez Whiz preferable to provolone? Should the steak be sliced thickly or chopped into a hash? The only thing everyone seems to agree on: the roll must be from Amoroso's Baking Company. The two best-known places, Pat's King of Steaks (1237 E. Passyunk Ave.) and Geno's Steaks (1219 South 9th St.), lie across the street from each other, making a personal taste-test very simple. Though Rick's Philly Steaks (in the Reading Terminal Market, 12th and Arch Sts.) offers chicken and vegetarian versions, no one can deny this place's authenticity—it's run by the grandson of Pat Olivieri, who claims to have invented the cheese steak in 1933. Wherever you go, be ready to give your order the right way—state your cheese choice first (usually "Whiz," provolone, or American), and say "wit" or "witout" to indicate your onion preference.

People either love or hate okra.

Okrafest

September

Checotah, Oklahoma

Notoriously slimy, okra is one of those veggies people either love or hate. Lovers won't want to miss this, one of the only okra celebrations in the United States. Okra-cooking contest winners serve a variety of dishes, which in the past have included pickled okra, okra dogs, okra gumbo, okra bread, and even okra ice cream. Sample free fried okra from the Okra Pot, which cooks more than 400 pounds of the pod. Antique tractors, an open car show, live music, and vendors round out the fest. *(918) 473-2070*

Idaho Spud Day

September

Shelley, Idaho

Bingham County grows more potatoes than any other county in the United States. So when harvest time comes around, there's good reason to celebrate—and to give out free baked potatoes. Spud Day isn't for couch potatoes. Competition is fierce in the spud-day activities, which feature a spud-picking contest as well as Spud Tug: After a cement mixer fills a pit with mashed potatoes, tug-of-war teams try to pull each other into the glop. There are also potato recipe contests and a kids' parade. *(208) 524-3880*

Persimmon Festival

September

Mitchell, Indiana

If you've never eaten a persimmon, you can make up for lost time at this week-long event. The people of Mitchell offer persimmon fudge, bread, cookies, cake, and ice cream, but the most popular dish is pudding. In fact, the Persimmon Pudding Contest grabs more attention than the midway rides, arts and crafts, and candlelight tours of Spring Mill State Park. When the festival's over and withdrawal sets in, don't get caught nabbing persimmons from anyone's tree—around these parts, that's a serious crime.

(812) 849-4441, www.mitchellpersimmonfestival.org

Barnesville Pumpkin Festival

September

Barnesville, Ohio

Maybe you've rolled a pumpkin before, but have you ever rolled one uphill with sticks? At Barnesville's fall extravaganza, you can compete against other pumpkin-pushers on a tough 50-foot course. After the race, treat yourself to pumpkin pancakes, pumpkin fudge, or maybe even a pumpkin shake. Don't miss the King Pumpkin contest—winning pumpkins have tipped the scales at more than 1,000 pounds. And FYI, that enormous orange thing looming overhead isn't the Great Pumpkin; it's Barnesville's water tower. *(740) 425-2593, www.barnesvillepumpkinfestival.com*

LOCAL DISH DETOUR

To: Louisville, Kentucky (60 miles SE of Mitchell)

In 1923, chef Fred Schmidt of the Brown Hotel in Louisville got tired of making the same old ham and eggs in the wee hours of the morning for patrons who needed sustenance after the hotel's nightly dinner-dance. So he created the hot brown, an open-faced turkey sandwich with bacon and a creamy parmesan cheese sauce. The Brown Hotel still serves the classic Hot Brown in its J. Graham's Café (335 W. Broadway), but it's also available in various incarnations at other restaurants around town. The quirkily furnished Lynn's Paradise Café (984 Barret Ave.) serves its rendition, the "Paradise Hot Brown," with a slice of cheddar on top.

LOCAL DISH DETOUR

To: Cincinnati, Ohio (213 miles SW Barnesville)

It's said that Cincinnati has more chili parlors than it does McDonald's. Most of those are outposts of two chains—Gold Star and Skyline, which both have their fans—but plenty of others thrive as well. At Empress Chili (locations include 8340 Vine St.), you can try the original recipe. This is where, in 1922, Tom Kiradjieff, a Macedonian immigrant, invented Cincinnati-style chili—spiced ground beef in tomato sauce ladled over spaghetti. He's also the one who started the custom of ordering it "two-way" (with spaghetti only), "three-way" (add grated cheese), "four-way" (add chopped onions), or "five-way" (add kidney beans). For a spicier version and 24-hour service, head to Camp Washington Chili (3005 Colerain Ave.), which won a Regional Classics Award from the James Beard Foundation. On the city's west side, Price Hill Chili (4920 Glenway Ave.) reigns; locals often gather here after high school football games to celebrate (or mourn) with a plate of coneys—small hot dogs topped with chili, onions, mustard, or cheese.

Naples Grape Festival

September

Naples, New York

Festival-goers can't get enough of the famous grape pies introduced in Naples in the 1950s. Over the years, entrants in the World's Greatest Grape Pie Contest have shocked traditionalists with new twists on Irene Bouchard's original recipe, introducing such radical additions as peanut butter and meringue (gasp!). After the judging, try a slice of a competing pie, then kick off your shoes and join in the Grape Stompin'—it's all about how much juice you produce.

(585) 374-2240, www.naplesgrapefest.org

Norsk Høstfest

October

Minot, North Dakota

North America's largest Scandinavian festival draws 65,000 people to Minot's sprawling All Seasons Arena, which is divided into separate halls representing Denmark, Finland, Iceland, Norway, and Sweden. Booths offer all things Scandinavian, from birchbark boxes and baskets to rune stones and reindeer skins. On stage there are yodelers, folk dancers, and top-name entertainers. For those who can't stomach lutefisk (cod soaked in lye and then boiled), there are other Scandinavian specialties like lefse, Swedish meatballs, and Danish kringle. *(701) 852-2368, www.hostfest.com*

Boggy Bayou Mullet Festival

October

Niceville, Florida

Elsewhere it might be scorned as "roadkill with fins," but the people who live along Boggy Bayou love the mullet. And they're out to make converts of the rest of us. They'll serve some 10 tons of the humble bottom feeder—oops, make that "algae eater"—during three days of mullet mania. If smoked or fried mullet doesn't tempt your taste buds, try other local specialties like crawfish bread, boiled peanuts, and alligator-on-a-stick. A parade, live entertainment, pony rides, and a ranger station with live wildlife add to the excitement.

(850) 729-4008, www.mulletfestival.com

Kona Coffee Cultural Festival

November

Kailua Kona, Hawaii

There's enough joe here to give anyone the jitters. Hawaii is the only state where coffee is grown commercially, and the Big Island's Kona Coast is renowned for its particularly flavorful bean. Watch as local growers brew their best coffee at the Cupping Contest, then try your hand harvesting beans in the Kona-picking competition. Pooped after all that picking? Stay awake by sampling different island coffees or indulging in a coffee-flavored dessert at the Kona Coffee Recipe Contest. *(808) 326-7820, www.konacoffeefest.com*

LOCAL DISH DETOUR

To: Atlantic City, New Jersey (41 miles S of Chatsworth)

Atlantic City was promoted in the 1800s as a resort for convalescents—a place where the salty sea breezes were reputed to cure everything from consumption to insanity. Now the city's reputation as the home of sticky-sweet saltwater taffy makes any health claims a little harder to justify. James' Candy Company (two locations including the Boardwalk at New York Avenue) has been in business since 1880. Its taffy purportedly doesn't stick to candy wrappers (or teeth). Flavors such as cinnamon and coconut can be purchased packaged in a retro souvenir papier-mâché barrel that doubles as a bank. James' also makes chocolate-covered taffy. Fralinger's Original Salt Water Taffy (two locations including 1325 Boardwalk) came along in 1885. The original flavors—chocolate, vanilla, and molasses—are still available, along with others such as peppermint, root beer, and lime. Both companies offer gift packages featuring saltwater taffy alongside other treats such as macaroons, peanut butter chews, and creamy after-dinner mints.

Chitlin' Strut

November

Salley, South Carolina

"Chitlin'" is Southern slang for "chitterling," a cleaned pig intestine floured and deep-fried in peanut oil. Folks stand in long lines to get their hands on the delicacy, which connoisseurs say tastes similar to pork rinds and has an addictive texture—a crunch followed by a savory chew. Even avid chitlin'-eaters agree that the sizzling intestines smell something awful, yet more than 10,000 lb. are devoured on festival day. After dinner, listen to the champs serenade the swine with their best "Sooooey!" at the "hawg-calling" contest. *(803) 258-3485, www.chitlinstrut.com*

Chatsworth Cranberry Festival

October

Chatsworth, New Jersey

Strap on your waders and jump into one of the dozens of cranberry bogs at the third-largest U.S. cranberry harvest. A cornucopia of cranberry creations, from cranberry mustard and cranberry vinegar to cranberry ice cream and cranberry upside-down cake, provide just the right blend of sweet and tart to satisfy any palate. *(609) 726-9237, www.cranfest.org*

LOCAL DISH DETOUR

To: Charleston, South Carolina (112 miles SE of Salley)

When slaves from West Africa arrived in Charleston, South Carolina, in the early 1700s, so did benne seeds, now more commonly known as sesame seeds. Benne seed wafers, now a local tradition, can be bought from many vendors in the downtown open-air shopping area known as the Market (Market St. between Meeting St. and E. Bay St.). One of the biggest purveyors of the treats is the Olde Colony Bakery (1391 B Stuart Engalls Blvd.) in nearby Mount Pleasant, which claims that its recipe is more than 100 years old. Back in Charleston, the Anson Restaurant (12 Anson St.) fancies up the tradition by forming the seed mixture into an edible basket and filling it with ice cream.

HOTEL RESOURCES

Adam's Mark Hotels & Resorts
(800) 444-2326
www.adamsmark.com

America's Best Inns & Suites
(800) 237-8466
www.americasbestinns.com

AmericInn
(800) 396-5007
www.americinn.com

Baymont Inn & Suites
(877) 229-6668
www.baymontinn.com

Best Western
(800) 780-7234
www.bestwestern.com

Budget Host
(800) 283-4678
www.budgethost.com

Clarion Hotels
(877) 424-6423
www.clarionhotel.com

Coast Hotels & Resorts
(800) 716-6199
www.coasthotels.com

Comfort Inn
(877) 424-6423
www.comfortinn.com

Comfort Suites
(877) 424-6423
www.comfortsuites.com

Courtyard by Marriott
(888) 236-2427
www.courtyard.com

Crowne Plaza Hotel & Resorts
(877) 227-6963
www.crowneplaza.com

Days Inn
(800) 329-7466
www.daysinn.com

Delta Hotels & Resorts
(888) 890-3222
www.deltahotels.com

Doubletree Hotels, Guest Suites, Resorts & Clubs
(800) 222-8733
www.doubletree.com

Drury Hotels
(800) 378-7946
www.druryhotels.com

Econo Lodge
(877) 424-6423
www.econolodge.com

Embassy Suites Hotels
(800) 362-2779
www.embassysuites.com

Extended Stay Hotels
(800) 804-3724
www.extstay.com

Fairfield Inn by Marriott
(800) 228-2800
www.fairfieldinn.com

Fairmont Hotels & Resorts
(800) 257-7544
www.fairmont.com

Four Points by Sheraton
(800) 368-7764
www.fourpoints.com

Four Seasons Hotels & Resorts
(800) 819-5053
www.fourseasons.com

Hampton Inn
(800) 426-7866
www.hamptoninn.com

Hilton Hotels
(800) 445-8667
www.hilton.com

Holiday Inn Hotels & Resorts
(888) 465-4329
www.holidayinn.com

Homewood Suites
(800) 225-5466
www.homewood-suites.com

Howard Johnson
(800) 446-4656
www.hojo.com

Hyatt Hotels & Resorts
(888) 591-1234
www.hyatt.com

InterContinental Hotels & Resorts
(888) 424-6835
www.intercontinental.com

Jameson Inns
(800) 526-3766
www.jamesoninns.com

Knights Inn
(800) 843-5644
www.knightsinn.com

La Quinta Inns & Suites
(800) 753-3757
www.lq.com

Le Méridien Hotels & Resorts
(800) 543-4300
www.lemeridien.com

Loews Hotels
(866) 563-9792
www.loewshotels.com

MainStay Suites
(877) 424-6423
www.mainstaysuites.com

Marriott International
(888) 236-2427
www.marriott.com

Microtel Inns & Suites
(800) 771-7171
www.microtelinn.com

Motel 6
(800) 466-8356
www.motel6.com

Omni Hotels
(888) 444-6664 (U.S. only)
(402) 952-6664 (outside U.S.)
www.omnihotels.com

Park Inn
(888) 201-1801
www.parkinn.com

Preferred Hotels & Resorts
(800) 323-7500
www.preferredhotels.com

Quality Inn & Suites
(877) 424-6423
www.qualityinn.com

Radisson Hotels & Resorts
(888) 201-1718
www.radisson.com

Ramada Worldwide
(800) 272-6232
www.ramada.com

Red Lion Hotels
(800) 733-5466
www.redlion.com

Red Roof Inn
(800) 733-7663
www.redroof.com

Renaissance Hotels & Resorts by Marriott
(800) 468-3571
www.renaissancehotels.com

Residence Inn by Marriott
(800) 331-3131
www.residenceinn.com

The Ritz-Carlton
(800) 542-8680
www.ritzcarlton.com

Rodeway Inn
(877) 424-6423
www.rodeway.com

Sheraton Hotels & Resorts
(800) 325-3535
www.sheraton.com

Sleep Inn
(877) 424-6423
www.sleepinn.com

Super 8
(800) 800-8000
www.super8.com

Travelodge Hotels
(800) 578-7878
www.travelodge.com

Westin Hotels & Resorts
(800) 937-8461
www.westin.com

Wyndham Hotels & Resorts
(877) 999-3223
www.wyndham.com

To find a bed-and-breakfast at your destination, log on to www.bedandbreakfast.com.®

NOTE: All toll-free reservation numbers are for the U.S. and Canada unless otherwise noted. These numbers were accurate at press time, but are subject to change. Find more listings or book a hotel online at randmcnally.com.

RENTAL CAR RESOURCES

Advantage Rent-A-Car
(800) 777-5500
www.arac.com

Alamo Rent A Car
(800) 462-5266
www.alamo.com

Avis Rent A Car
(800) 331-1212
www.avis.com

Budget Rent A Car
(800) 527-0700
(U.S. & Canada)
(800) 472-3325
(International)
www.budget.com

Enterprise Rent-A-Car
(800) 261-7331
www.enterprise.com

Hertz Car Rental
(800) 654-3131
(U.S. & Canada)
(800) 654-3001
(International)
www.hertz.com

National Car Rental
(800) 227-7368
www.nationalcar.com

Payless Car Rental
(800) 729-5377
(U.S., Canada & Mexico)
www.paylesscarrental.com

Thrifty Car Rental
(800) 847-4389
www.thrifty.com

CELL PHONE EMERGENCY NUMBERS

Alabama *47
Alaska 911
Arizona 911
Arkansas 911
California 911
Colorado 911; *277
Connecticut 911
Delaware 911
District of Columbia 911
Florida 911; *347
Georgia 911; *477
Hawaii 911
Idaho *477

Illinois 911
Indiana 911
Iowa 911; *55
Kansas 911; *47
Kentucky (800) 222-5555 (in KY)
Louisiana 911; *577 (road emergencies)
Maine 911
Maryland 911
Massachusetts 911
Michigan 911
Minnesota 911
Mississippi 911
Missouri *55

Montana 911
Nebraska *55
Nevada *647
New Hampshire *77
New Jersey 911, *77
New Mexico 911
New York 911
North Carolina 911; *47
North Dakota *2121
Ohio 911
Oklahoma 911
Oregon 911
Pennsylvania 911

Rhode Island 911
South Carolina 911
South Dakota 911
Tennessee 911; *847
Texas 911
Utah 911; *11
Vermont 911
Virginia 911
Washington 911
West Virginia 911; *77
Wisconsin 911
Wyoming 911

Map Legend

Roads and related symbols
- Free limited-access highway
- Toll limited-access highway
- New road (under construction as of press time)
- Other multilane highway
- Principal highway
- Other through highway
- Other road (conditions vary — local inquiry suggested)
- Unpaved road (conditions vary — local inquiry suggested)
- One way route; ferry
- Interstate highway; Interstate highway business route
- U.S. highway; U.S. highway business route
- Trans-Canada highway; Autoroute
- Mexican highway or Central American highway
- State or provincial highway
- Secondary state, secondary provincial, or county highway
- County trunk highway
- Toll booth or fee booth
- Tunnel; mountain pass
- Interchanges and exit numbers (For most states, the mileage between interchanges may be determined by subtracting one number from the other.)
- Highway miles between arrows (Segments of one mile or less not shown.)
- Comparative distance 1 mile = 1.609 kilometers 1 kilometer = 0.621 mile

Cities & towns (size of type on map indicates relative population)
- National capital; state or provincial capital
- County seat or independent city
- City, town, or recognized place; neighborhood
- Urbanized area
- Separate cities within metropolitan area

Parks, recreation areas, & points of interest
- U.S. or Canadian national park
- U.S. or Canadian national monument, other National Park Service facility, state or provincial park, or recreation area
- Park with camping facilities; park without camping facilities
- National forest, national grassland, or city park; wildlife refuge
- Point of interest, historic site or monument
- Airport
- Campsite; golf course or country club
- Hospital or medical center
- Indian reservation
- Information center or Tourist Information Center (T.I.C.)
- Military or governmental installation; military airport

Physical features
- Dam
- Mountain peak; highest point in state/province
- Lake; dry lake
- River; intermittent river
- Desert; glacier
- Swamp or mangrove swamp

Other symbols
- Area shown in greater detail on inset map
- Inset map page indicator
- Intracoastal waterway
- County or parish boundary and name
- State or provincial boundary
- National boundary
- Continental divide
- Time zone boundary

Population figures are from the latest available census or are Census Bureau or Rand McNally estimates.

For a complete list of abbreviations that appear on the maps, visit go.randmcnally.com/ABBR.

©2010 Rand McNally

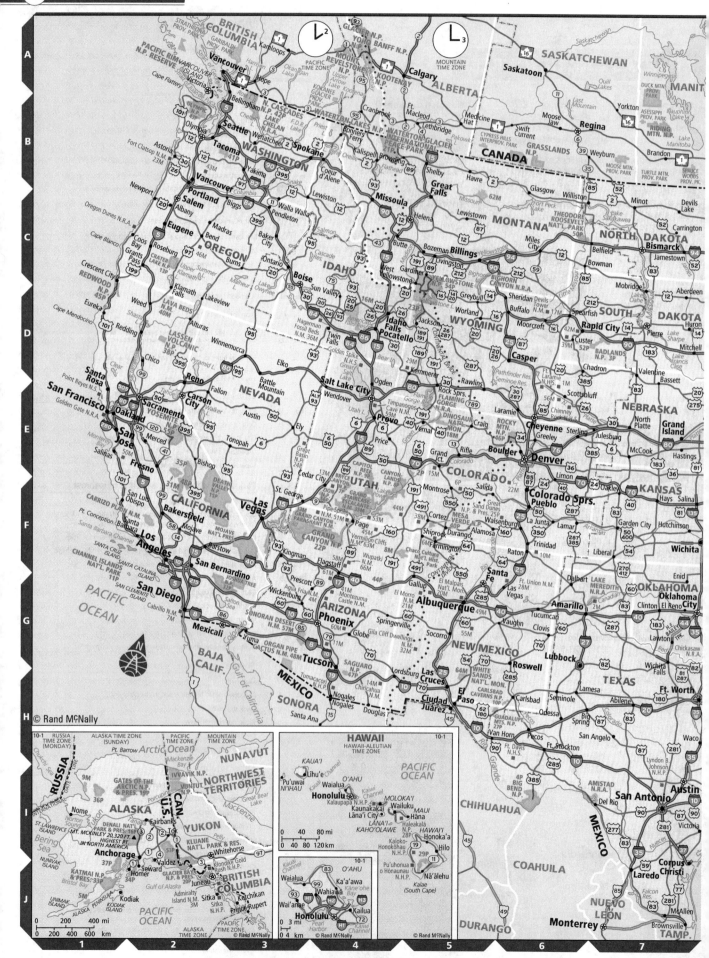

© Rand McNally

Alabama

Population: 4,627,851
Land area: 50,744 sq. mi.
Capital: Montgomery

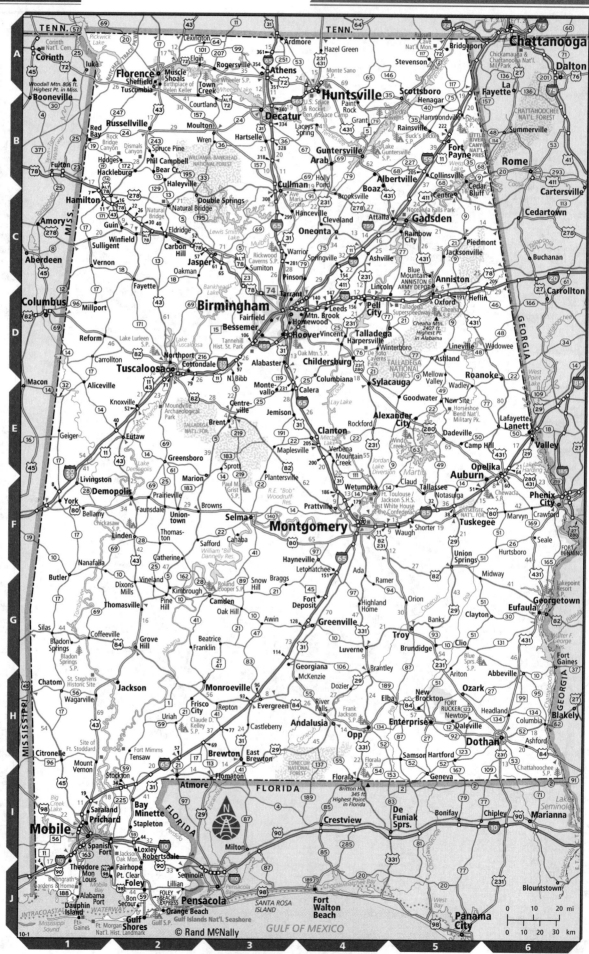

© Rand McNally

10-1

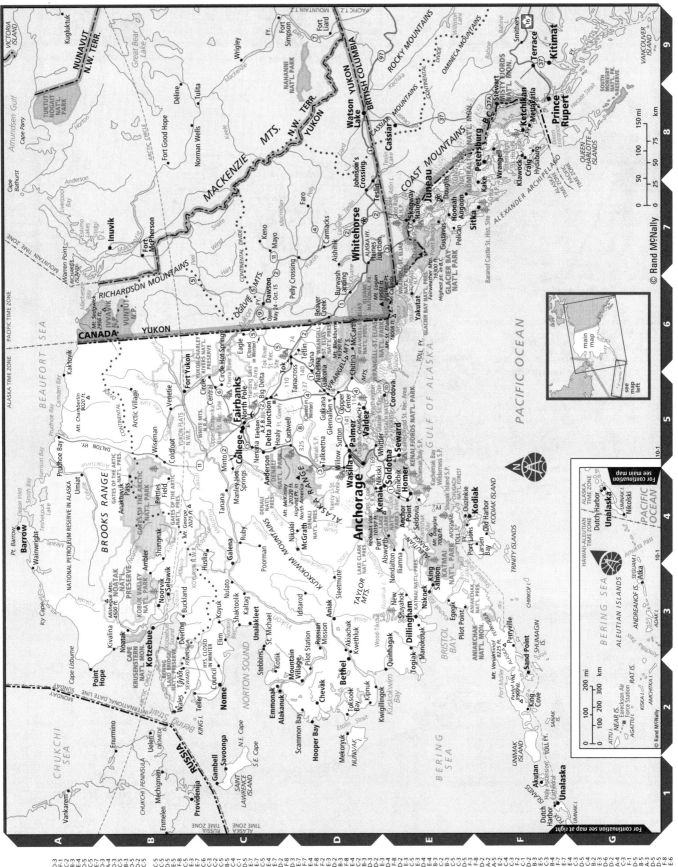

© Rand McNally

N

For continuation see map at right

For continuation see main map

Alaska

Population: 683,478
Land area: 571,951 sq. mi.
Capital: Juneau

Cities and Towns

Akiachak	D-3
Akutan	F-1
Alakanuk	B-3
Ambler	B-4
Anchor Point	D-5
Anchorage	D-5
Anderson	C-5
Angoon	E-7
Aniak	A-4
Barrow	A-4
Bethel	D-3
Big Delta	D-5
Buckland	B-3
Cantwell	D-5
Chevak	C-3
Circle	C-5
Circle Hot Springs	
Station	C-5
College	C-5
Copper Center	D-5
Cordova	E-6
Craig	F-8
Delta Junction	C-5
Dillingham	D-3
Douglas	E-7
Eagle	C-6
Emmonak	B-3
Fairbanks	C-5
Fort Yukon	B-5
Galena	C-4
Gambell	C-2
Glennallen	D-5
Gustavus	E-7
Haines	E-7
Healy	C-5
Homer	D-5
Hoonah	E-7
Hooper Bay	D-2
Idita rog	C-4
Juneau	E-7
Kake	E-7
Kenai	D-5
Ketchikan	F-8
King Cove	F-2
King Salmon	D-3
Kipnuk	D-2
Kivalina	B-3
Klawock	F-8
Kodiak	E-4
Kotlik	B-3
Kotzebue	B-3
Kwethluk	D-3
Kwigillingok	D-3
Manokotak	D-3
McGrath	C-4
Metlakatla	F-8
Mountain Village	C-3
Naknek	D-3
Nenana	C-5
New Stuyahok	D-3
Nikiski	D-5
Ninilchik	D-4
Noatak	B-3
Nome	C-2
Noorvik	B-3
Nulato	C-4
North Pole	C-5
Palmer	D-5
Perryville	E-3
Petersburg	E-7
Pilot Station	C-3
Point Hope	B-2
Prudhoe Bay	A-5
Quinhagak	D-3
Ruby	C-4
St. Michael	C-3
Savoonga	C-1
Scammon Bay	C-3
Selawik	B-3
Seward	D-5
Sitka	E-7
Skagway	E-7
Soldotna	D-5
Stebbins	C-3
Talkeetna	D-5
Teller	B-2
Togiak	D-3
Tok	C-6
Toksook Bay	D-3
Umiat	A-4
Unalakleet	C-3
Unalaska	F-1
Valdez	D-5
Venetie	B-5
Wainwright	A-3
Wasilla	D-5
Willow	D-5
Wrangell	E-7
Yakutat	E-6

For border crossing information,
please see p. 59

Get more Arizona info at go.randmcnally.com/AZ

Arizona

Population: 6,338,755
Land area: 113,635 sq. mi.
Capital: Phoenix

Cities and Towns

© Rand McNally

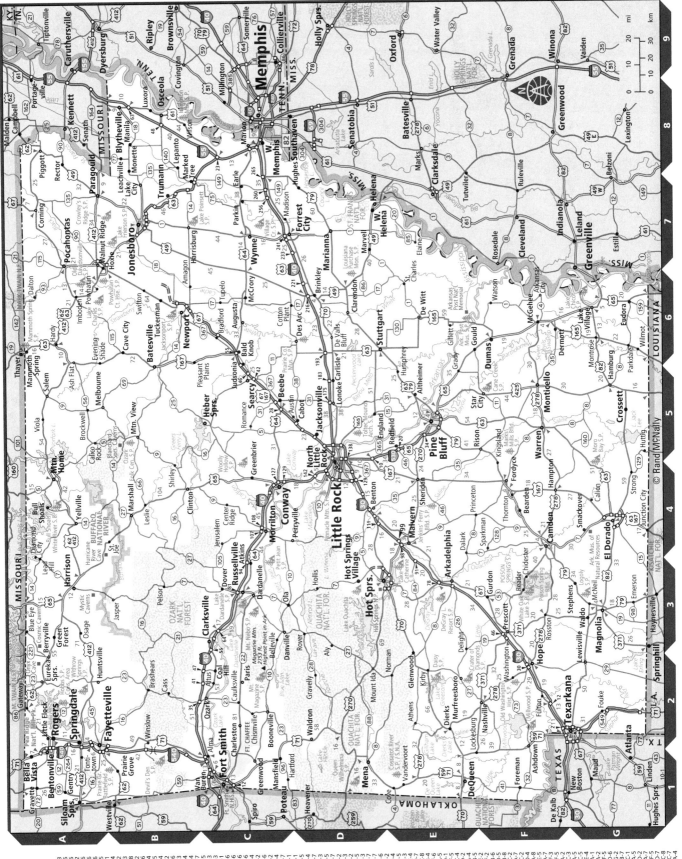

Arkansas

Population: 2,834,797
Land area: 52,068 sq. mi.
Capital: Little Rock

Cities and Towns

California
Population: 36,553,215
Land area: 155,959 sq. mi.
Capital: Sacramento

Cities and Towns

For border crossing information, please see p. 59

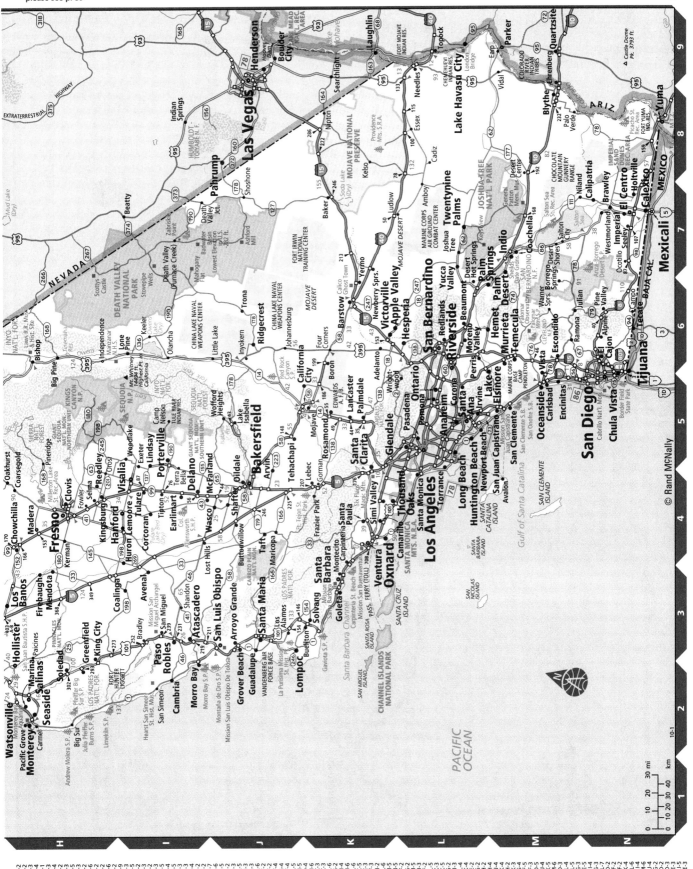

© Rand McNally

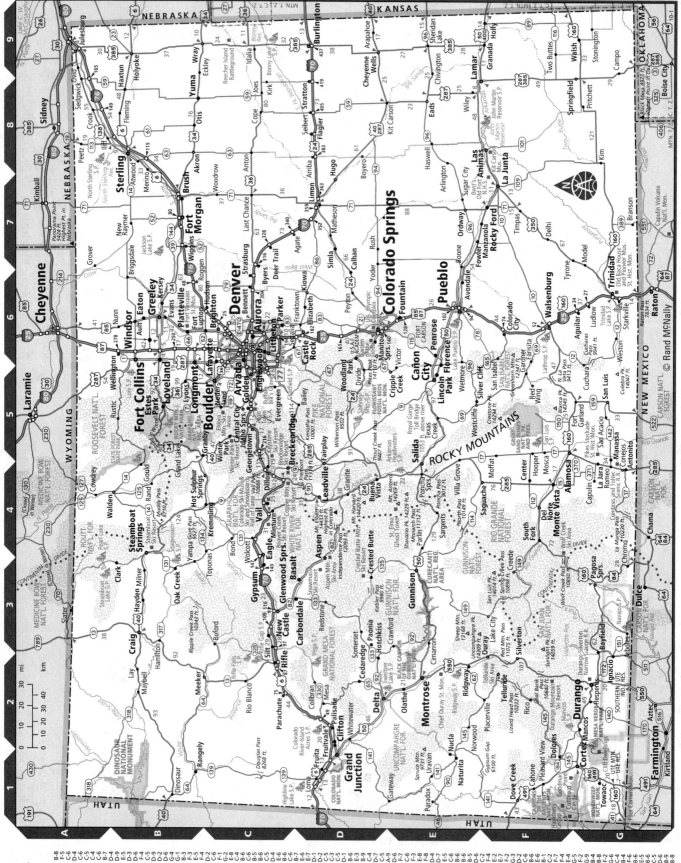

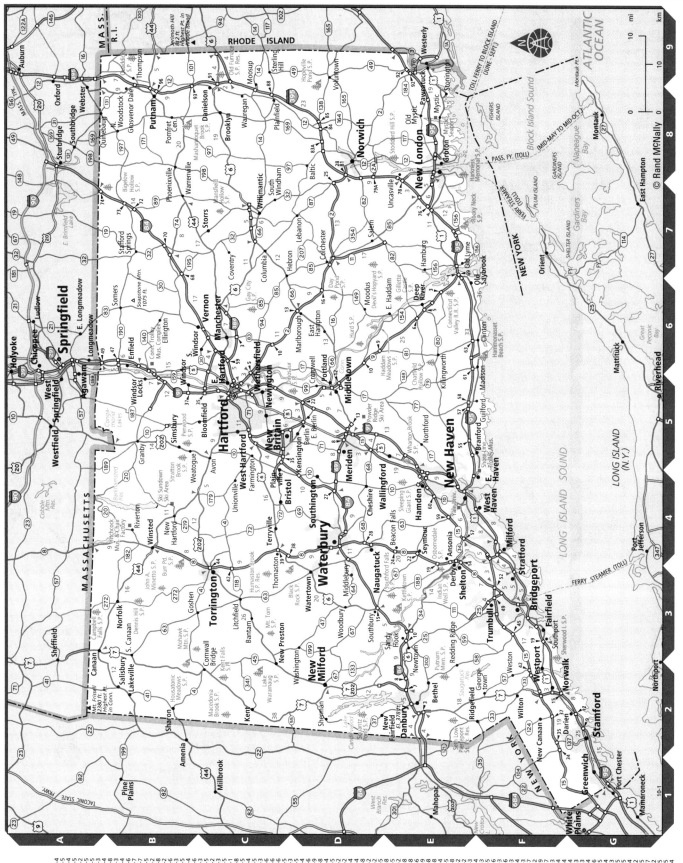

Connecticut

Population: 3,502,309
Land area: 4,845 sq. mi.
Capital: Hartford

Cities and Towns

Ansonia E-4
Avon C-5
Beacon Falls E-4
Berlin D-5
Bethel F-2
Bloomfield C-5
Bridgeport F-3
Bristol D-4
Brooklyn A-3
Canaan D-7
Cheshire E-4
Clinton C-7
Colchester C-7
Coventry C-6
Cromwell D-5
Danbury F-2
Danielson B-8
Darien F-3
Deep River C-7
East Hartford C-5
East Haven E-4
Enfield B-5
Fairfield F-3
Farmington C-5
Georgetown F-3
Granby B-5
Greenwich G-1
Groton E-8
Guilford E-6
Hamden E-4
Hartford C-5
Litchfield D-3
Madison E-6
Manchester C-6
Marlborough C-6
Meriden D-5
Middlebury E-4
Middletown D-6
Milford F-4
Moodus C-6
Moosup B-9
Mystic E-8
Naugatuck E-4
New Britain D-5
New Canaan F-2
New Fairfield F-2
New Hartford C-4
New Haven E-4
New London E-8
New Milford E-2
New Preston D-2
Newington D-5
Newtown F-2
Norfolk C-3
Northford E-5
Norwalk F-3
Norwich D-8
Old Mystic E-8
Old Saybrook D-7
Pawcatuck E-9
Plainfield B-8
Plainville D-4
Portland D-6
Putnam A-9
Ridgefield F-2
Salisbury D-3
Sandy Hook E-2
Seymour E-4
Shelton E-3
Simsbury C-5
Somers B-6
South Canaan D-7
South Windsor C-5
Southbury E-3
Southington D-5
Stafford Springs B-6
Stamford G-2
Sterling Hill B-8
Storrs C-6
Stratford F-3
Terryville D-4
Thomaston D-4
Torrington C-4
Trumbull F-3
Unionville C-5
Vernon C-6
Wallingford D-5
Waterbury E-4
Watertown D-4
West Hartford C-5
West Haven E-4
Westport F-3
Wethersfield C-5
Willimantic C-7
Wilton F-2
Winsted C-4
Windsor C-5
Windsor Locks B-5

Delaware

Population: 864,764
Land area: 1,954 sq. mi.
Capital: Dover

Cities and Towns

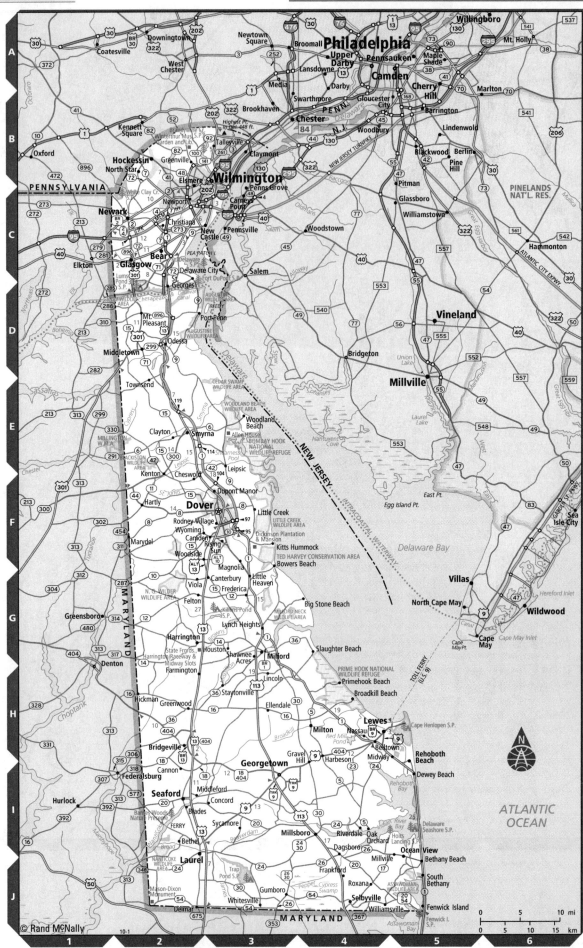

© Rand McNally

Florida

Population: 18,251,243
Land area: 53,927 sq. mi.
Capital: Tallahassee

© Rand McNally

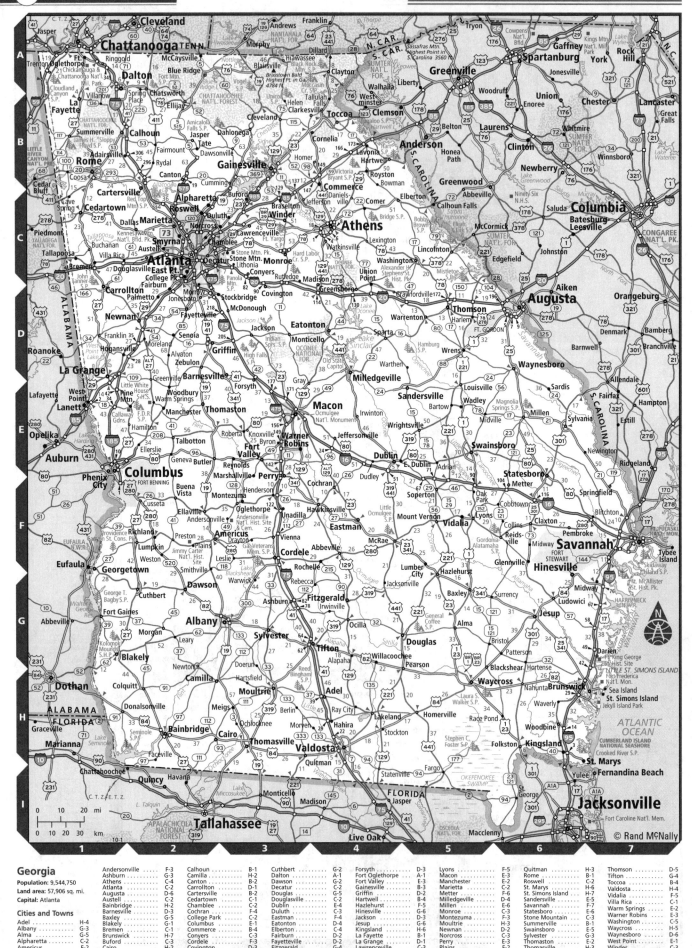

© Rand McNally

Georgia

Population: 9,544,750
Land area: 57,906 sq. mi.
Capital: Atlanta

Cities and Towns

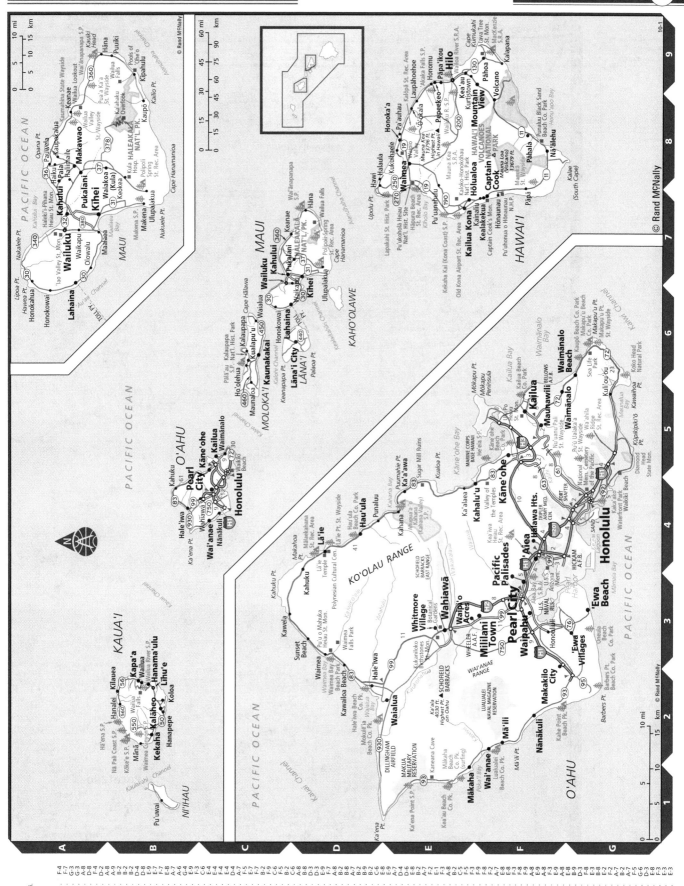

Hawaii

Population: 1,283,388
Land area: 6,423 sq. mi.
Capital: Honolulu

© Rand McNally

For border crossing information, please see p. 59

Idaho

Population: 1,499,402
Land area: 82,747 sq. mi.
Capital: Boise

Cities and Towns

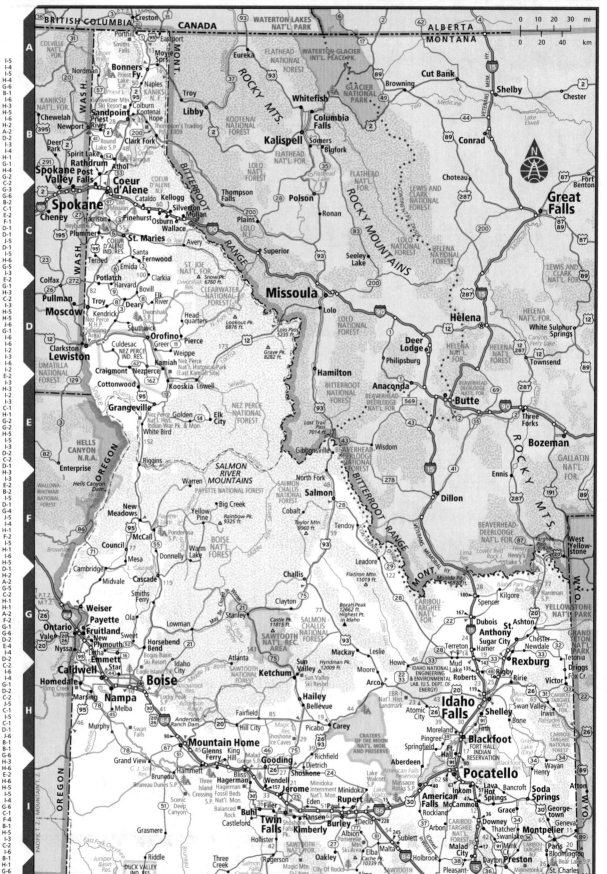

© Rand McNally

10-1

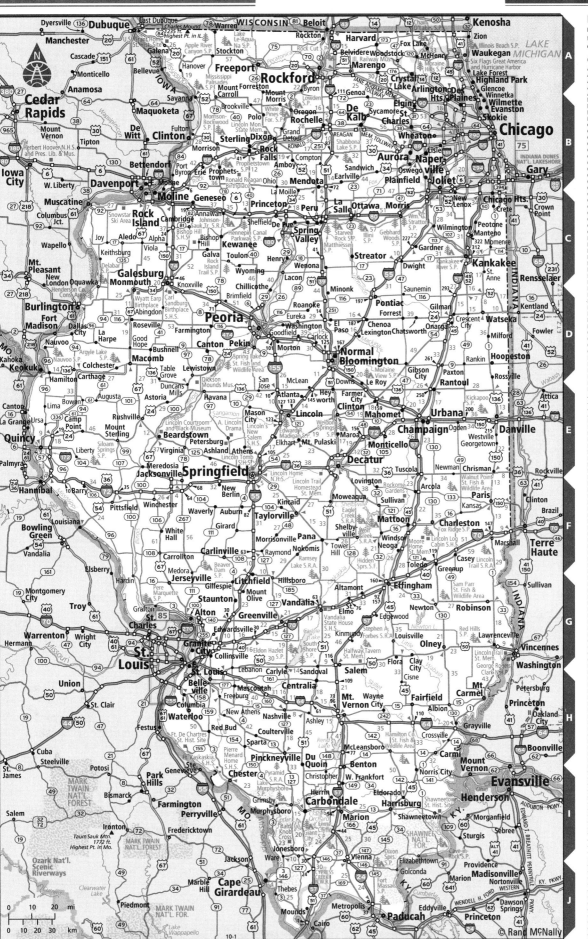

Illinois

Population: 12,852,548
Land area: 55,584 sq. mi.
Capital: Springfield

© Rand McNally

Indiana

Population: 6,345,289
Land area: 35,867 sq. mi.
Capital: Indianapolis

Cities and Towns

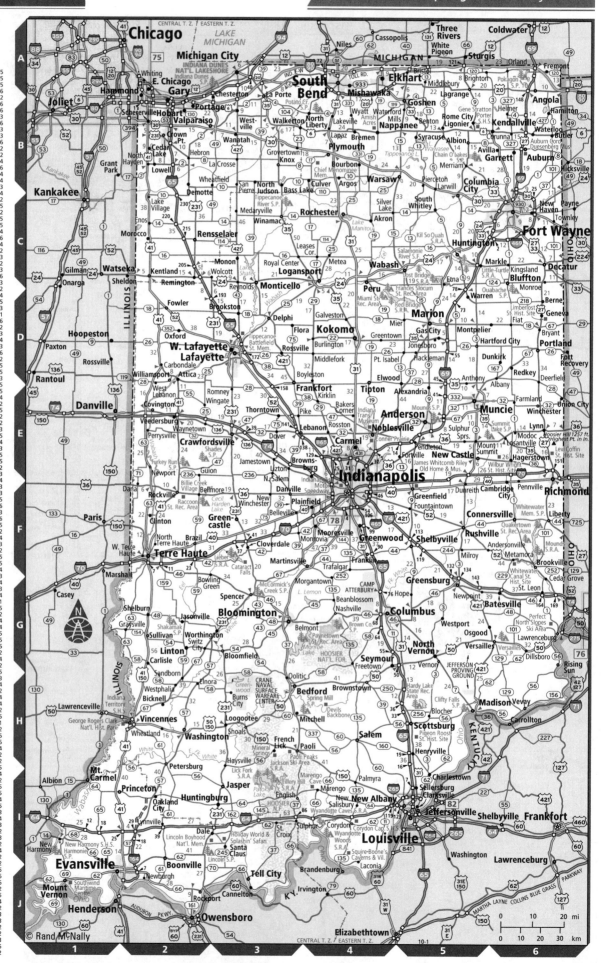

© Rand McNally

Iowa

Population: 2,988,046
Land area: 55,869 sq. mi.
Capital: Des Moines

Cities and Towns

City	Grid
Adel	D-5
Albia	E-6
Algona	B-4
Allison	B-6
Amana	D-7
Ames	C-5
Anamosa	C-8
Ankeny	D-5
Atlantic	D-3
Audubon	D-3
Bedford	F-4
Belle Plaine	C-7
Bettendorf	D-9
Bloomfield	F-7
Boone	C-5
Burlington	E-8
Carroll	C-3
Cedar Falls	B-7
Cedar Rapids	C-8
Centerville	C-5
Chariton	C-8
Charles City	D-5
Clarinda	D-3
Clarion	F-4
Clear Lake	B-5
Clinton	D-9
Coon Rapids	C-8
Corning	F-7
Corydon	F-8
Council Bluffs	C-3
Cresco	C-7
Creston	D-8
Dakota City	F-6
Davenport	E-6
De Witt	D-5
Decorah	D-3
Denison	D-3
Des Moines	D-7
Dubuque	D-9
Dyersville	D-4
Eagle Grove	B-5
Eldora	C-6
Elkader	A-7
Emmetsburg	B-4
Estherville	A-4
Fairfield	B-4
Forest City	D-9
Fort Dodge	A-7
Garner	B-5
Glenwood	C-8
Greenfield	C-8
Grinnell	D-6
Griswold	C-8
Grundy Center	B-5
Guthrie Center	D-4
Guttenberg	B-8
Hamburg	A-4
Hampton	E-7
Harlan	A-5
Humboldt	B-5
Ida Grove	D-7
Independence	D-6
Indianola	C-4
Iowa Falls	C-6
Jefferson	B-8
Keokuk	F-7
Keosauqua	D-4
Knoxville	C-6
Le Claire	D-8
Le Mars	B-6
Leon	D-3
Logan	B-4
Maquoketa	B-8
Marengo	D-7
Marion	E-8
Marshalltown	D-8
Mason City	B-7
McGregor	C-6
Missouri Valley	F-7
Montezuma	D-4
Monticello	D-9
Mount Ayr	B-2
Mount Pleasant	F-5
Mount Vernon	D-2
Muscatine	B-8
Nevada	C-8
New Hampton	C-6
Newton	A-6
North Liberty	D-6
Oelwein	C-4
Onawa	D-4
Orange City	C-2
Osage	A-6
Osceola	E-8
Oskaloosa	D-8
Ottumwa	E-7
Pella	D-4
Perry	C-5
Pocahontas	B-3
Primghar	A-3
Red Oak	D-8
Rock Rapids	C-4
Rockwell City	A-6
Sac City	C-2
Sheldon	C-3
Shenandoah	A-6
Sibley	A-2
Sidney	F-2
Sioux Center	B-2
Sioux City	C-2
Spencer	A-3
Spirit Lake	A-3
State Center	C-6
Storm Lake	B-3
Story City	C-5
Tama	C-6
Tipton	D-8
Toledo	C-6
Vinton	C-7
Wapello	E-8
Washington	D-8
Waterloo	C-7
Waukon	A-8
Waverly	B-7
Webster City	C-5
West Branch	D-8
West Liberty	D-8
West Union	B-7
Wilton	D-8
Winterset	E-5

© Rand McNally

Kansas

Population: 2,775,997
Land area: 81,815 sq. mi.
Capital: Topeka

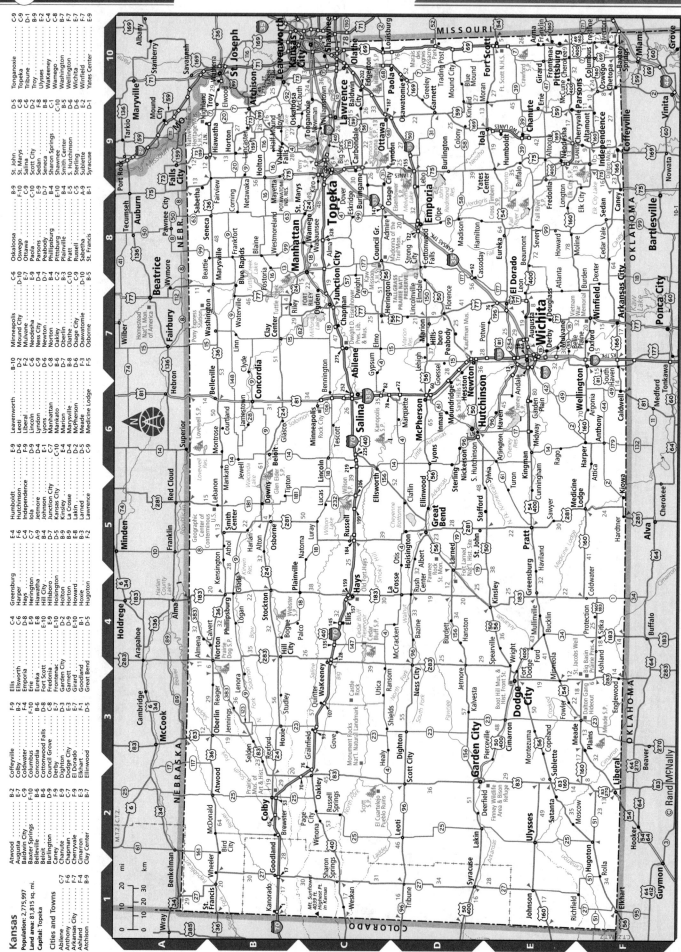

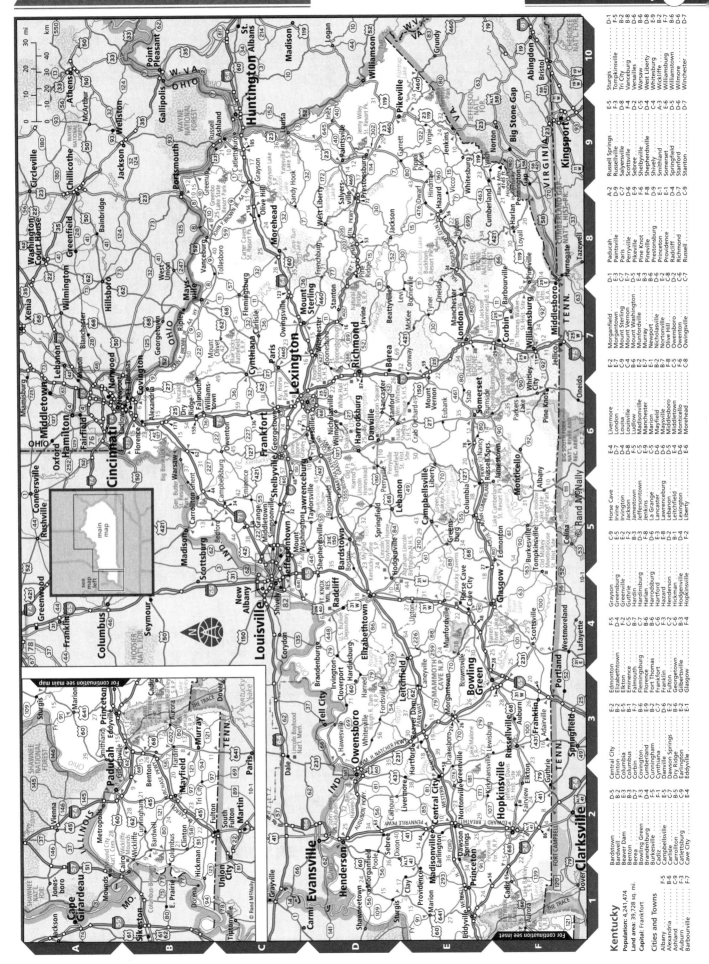

© Rand McNally

© Rand McNally

GULF OF MEXICO

Louisiana
Population: 4,293,204
Land area: 43,562 sq. mi.
Capital: Baton Rouge

Cities and Towns

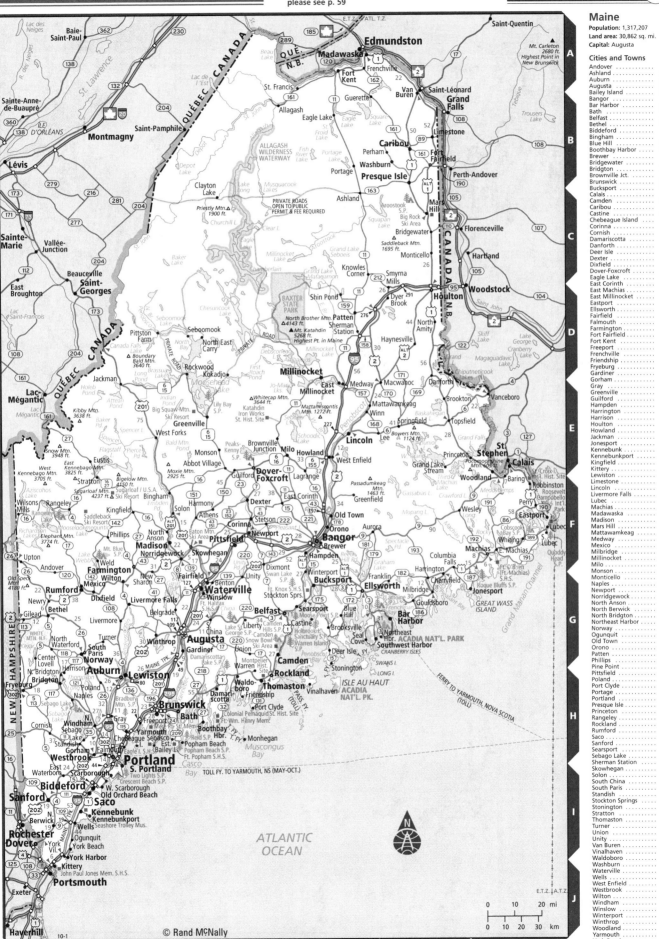

Maine

Population: 1,317,207
Land area: 30,862 sq. mi.
Capital: Augusta

Cities and Towns

© Rand McNally

Maryland

Population: 5,618,344
Land area: 9,774 sq. mi.
Capital: Annapolis

Cities and Towns

District of Columbia

Population:
588,292
Land area: 61 sq. mi.

City

© Rand McNally

10-1

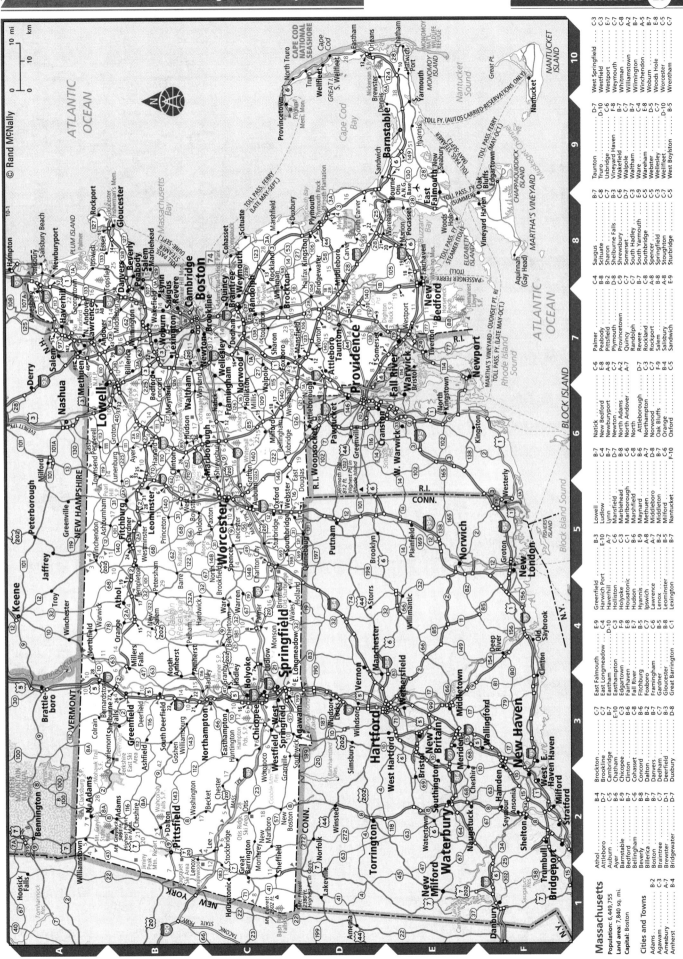

Massachusetts

Population 6,449,755
Land area: 7,840 sq. mi.
Capital: Boston

Cities and Towns

Adams	B-2
Agawam	C-3
Amesbury	A-7
Amherst	B-4
Athol	B-4
Attleboro	D-7
Auburn	C-5
Ayer	B-6
Barnstable	E-9
Bedford	B-7
Bellingham	D-6
Beverly	B-8
Billerica	B-7
Boston	C-7
Braintree	C-7
Bridgewater	D-7
Brockton	C-7
Brookline	C-7
Cambridge	C-7
Chatham	D-10
Chicopee	C-3
Cohasset	C-8
Concord	B-7
Dalton	C-6
Danvers	B-8
Deerfield	B-7
Duxbury	C-8
East Falmouth	E-9
East Longmeadow	C-4
Eastham	D-10
Easthampton	C-3
Edgartown	E-8
Fall River	C-8
Fitchburg	B-6
Foxboro	B-2
Framingham	C-7
Gloucester	B-8
Great Barrington	C-1
Greenfield	E-9
Harwich Port	C-4
Haverhill	D-10
Holliston	C-7
Holyoke	C-3
Housatonic	C-2
Hudson	B-6
Hyannis	E-9
Ipswich	B-7
Lawrence	A-8
Lenox	C-2
Leominster	B-5
Lexington	C-1
Lowell	B-3
Ludlow	E-10
Lynn	A-7
Mansfield	D-7
Marblehead	C-6
Marlborough	C-1
Marshfield	C-6
Maynard	B-6
Methuen	E-9
Middleboro	A-8
Middleton	D-8
Milford	B-5
Nantucket	B-7
Natick	B-7
New Bedford	C-4
Newton	B-7
North Adams	B-8
North Andover	C-6
North Attleborough	C-8
Northampton	A-3
Norton	A-8
Oak Bluffs	C-7
Orange	C-6
Oxford	F-10
Palmer	C-6
Peabody	E-8
Pittsfield	C-7
Provincetown	B-10
Quincy	A-2
Randolph	B-7
Revere	C-7
Rockland	E-8
Rockport	C-7
Salem	C-7
Salisbury	B-4
Sandwich	C-5
Saugus	C-4
Scituate	B-8
Sharon	B-3
Shelburne Falls	C-9
Shrewsbury	C-7
Somerset	C-6
South Hadley	C-3
Southbridge	C-5
Spencer	A-8
Springfield	C-7
Stoughton	A-8
Sturbridge	E-9
Taunton	D-7
Truro	C-8
Uxbridge	C-6
Vineyard Haven	B-3
Wakefield	C-9
Walpole	C-7
Waltham	A-2
Ware	B-7
Wareham	E-4
Webster	C-5
Wellesley	C-7
Wellfleet	D-10
West Boylston	B-5
West Springfield	C-3
Westfield	C-3
Westport	E-7
Weymouth	C-8
Whitman	B-7
Williamstown	A-2
Wilmington	B-7
Winchendon	A-5
Woburn	B-7
Woods Hole	D-5
Worcester	C-6
Wrentham	C-7

© Rand McNally

For border crossing information, please see p. 59

Explore Michigan at go.randmcnally.com/MI

Michigan

Population: 10,071,822
Land area: 56,804 sq. mi.
Capital: Lansing

Cities and Towns

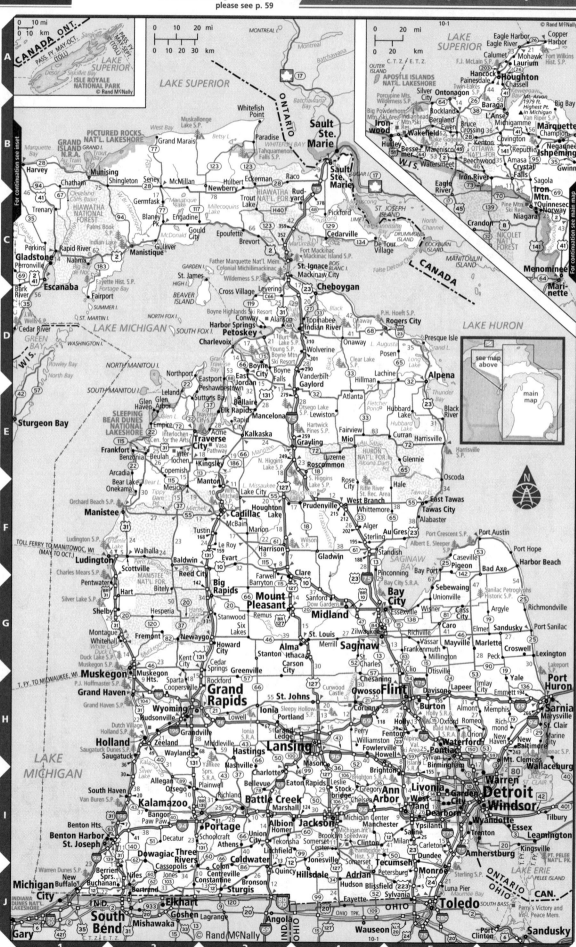

© Rand McNally

For border crossing information,
please see p. 59

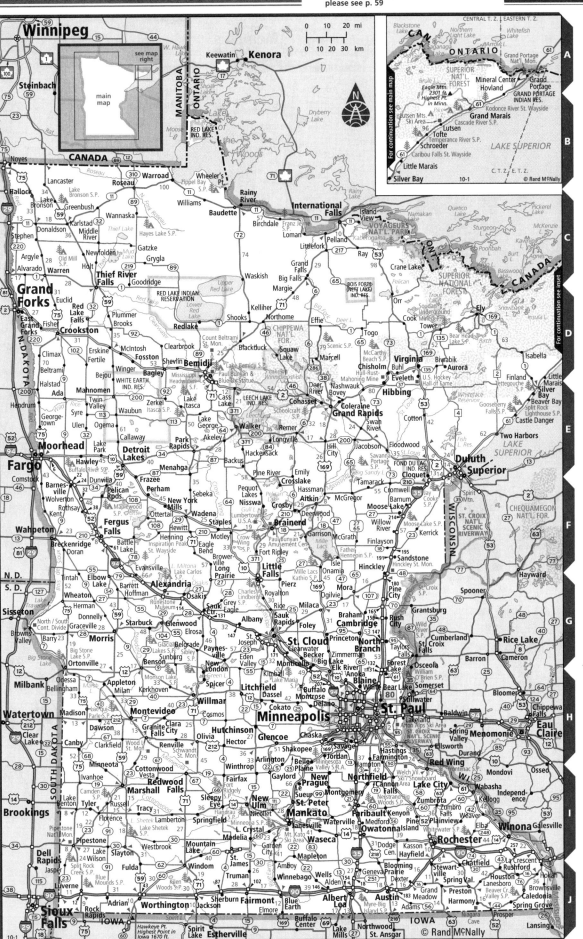

Minnesota

Population: 5,197,621
Land area: 79,610 sq. mi.
Capital: St. Paul

Cities and Towns

© Rand McNally

Mississippi

Population: 2,918,785
Land area: 46,907 sq. mi.
Capital: Jackson

Cities and Towns

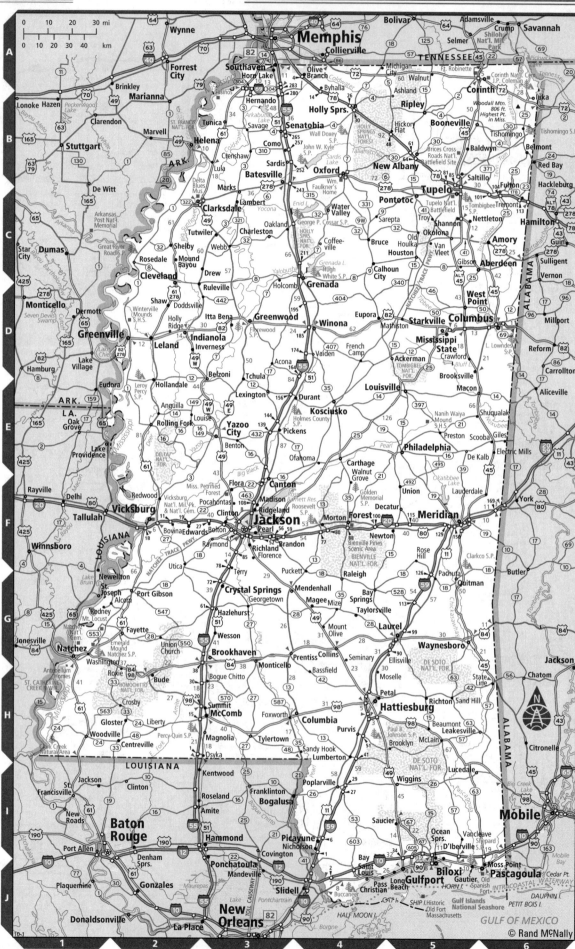

© Rand McNally

Missouri

Population: 5,878,415
Land area: 68,886 sq. mi.
Capital: Jefferson City

Cities and Towns

Arnold	D-7
Aurora	F-3
Ava	F-4
Belton	C-2
Bethany	A-3
Blue Springs	C-2
Bolivar	E-4
Bonne Terre	E-7
Boonville	D-5
Bowling Green	B-6
Branson	F-4
Brookfield	B-4
Butler	D-2
California	D-5
Cape Girardeau	F-8
Caruthersville	G-8
Carthage	F-3
Centralia	C-5
Charleston	F-8
Chillicothe	B-3
Columbia	C-5
Crystal City	D-7
De Soto	D-7
Dexter	F-8
East Prairie	F-8
El Dorado Springs	E-3
Eureka	D-7
Eveningshade	E-8
Excelsior Springs	C-2
Farmington	E-7
Festus	D-7
Fredericktown	E-7
Fulton	C-5
Gideon	G-8
Grandview	C-2
Hannibal	B-6
Harrisonville	C-2
Hayti	G-8
Independence	C-2
Jackson	F-8
Jefferson City	D-5
Joplin	F-2
Kennett	G-8
Kansas City	C-2
Kirksville	A-4
Lamar	E-3
Lebanon	E-5
Lexington	C-3
Liberty	C-2
Louisiana	B-6
Macon	B-5
Malden	G-8
Marshall	C-4
Maryville	A-2
Mexico	C-5
Moberly	B-5
Monett	F-3
Mountain Grove	F-5
Mount Vernon	F-3
Neosho	F-2
Nevada	E-3
New Madrid	G-8
Nixa	F-4
Odessa	C-3
Osage Beach	D-5
Ozark	F-4
Pacific	D-6
Palmyra	B-6
Perryville	E-8
Piedmont	F-7
Platte City	C-2
Pleasant Hill	C-2
Poplar Bluff	F-7
Potosi	E-7
Republic	F-4
Richmond	C-3
Rolla	D-6
St. Charles	C-7
St. James	D-6
St. Joseph	B-2
St. Louis	C-7
Ste. Genevieve	E-7
Salem	E-6
Sedalia	D-4
Sikeston	F-8
Springfield	F-4
Sullivan	D-6
Trenton	B-3
Troy	C-6
Union	D-6
Warrensburg	C-3
Warrenton	C-6
Washington	D-6
Waynesville	E-5
Webb City	F-2
Wentzville	C-6
West Plains	F-6
Windsor	D-3

For border crossing information, please see p. 59

Plan a Montana trip at go.randmcnally.com/MT

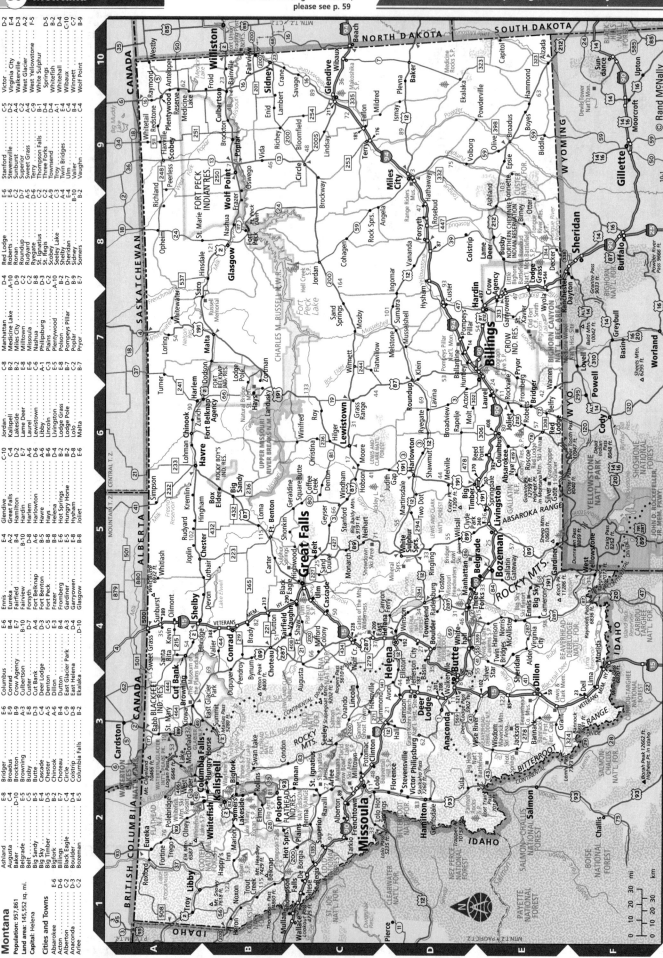

Montana

Population: 957,861
Land area: 145,552 sq. mi.
Capital: Helena

Cities and Towns

Absarokee	E-6
Acton	D-6
Alberton	D-3
Anaconda	D-3
Arlee	C-2

Ashland	E-8
Augusta	C-4
Belgrade	D-10
Belt	C-5
Big Sandy	B-5
Big Sky	E-4
Bigfork	B-2
Bigtimber	B-2
Billings	E-6
Black Eagle	C-4
Boulder	D-3
Bozeman	C-2

Bridger	E-6
Broadus	E-9
Brockton	B-9
Browning	A-3
Busby	E-8
Butte	D-3
Cascade	B-4
Chester	A-4
Choteau	B-2
Chinook	B-2
Circle	C-9
Colstrip	E-7
Columbia Falls	B-2

Columbus	E-6
Conrad	B-4
Crow Agency	A-3
Culbertson	B-10
Curt Bank	C-2
Custer	D-7
Deer Lodge	A-4
Dillon	D-3
Dutton	A-4
East Glacier Park	A-3
East Helena	D-4
Ekalaka	D-10

Ennis	E-6
Eureka	E-9
Fairfield	B-4
Fairview	B-10
Forsyth	D-7
Fort Belknap	A-6
Fort Benton	A-6
Fromberg	B-2
Gardiner	A-3
Garryowen	D-4
Glasgow	D-10

Glendive	E-4
Great Falls	B-4
Hamilton	B-2
Hardin	C-2
Harlem	B-5
Harlowton	D-3
Havre	A-6
Hays	A-5
Helena	B-3
Hot Springs	E-6
Hysham	E-8
Joliet	B-8

Jordan	C-8
Kalispell	B-2
Lakeside	B-2
Lame Deer	E-7
Laurel	A-6
Lewistown	A-6
Libby	A-6
Lincoln	C-6
Livingston	B-2
Lodge Grass	B-2
Lodge Pole	D-8
Lolo	E-6
Malta	E-6

Manhattan	C-8
Medicine Lake	B-2
Miles City	B-2
Milltown	D-7
Missoula	C-6
Nashua	C-2
Philipsburg	A-1
Plains	A-9
Polson	C-3
Poplar	B-8
Pompeys Pillar	B-8
Pryor	C-2

Red Lodge	D-4
Roberts	A-10
Ronan	C-2
Rudyard	D-7
Ryegate	A-5
St. Ignatius	C-2
St. Regis	A-9
Scobey	C-2
Seeley Lake	A-6
Shelby	E-8
Sheridan	B-7
Sidney	B-9
Somers	E-7

Stanford	C-5
Stevensville	E-6
Sunburst	C-7
Sweet Grass	A-2
Superior	B-1
Thompson Falls	B-1
Three Forks	D-4
Townsend	B-2
Troy	A-1
Whitefish	C-7
Whitehall	B-4
Valier	C-4

Victor	D-2
Virginia City	E-4
Walkerville	D-3
West Glacier	A-2
West Yellowstone	F-5
White Sulphur Springs	D-5
Whitefish	A-2
Whitehall	D-4
Troy	A-1
Winnett	B-4
Wibaux	C-10
Wolf Point	C-7
Vaughn	B-4
	A-9

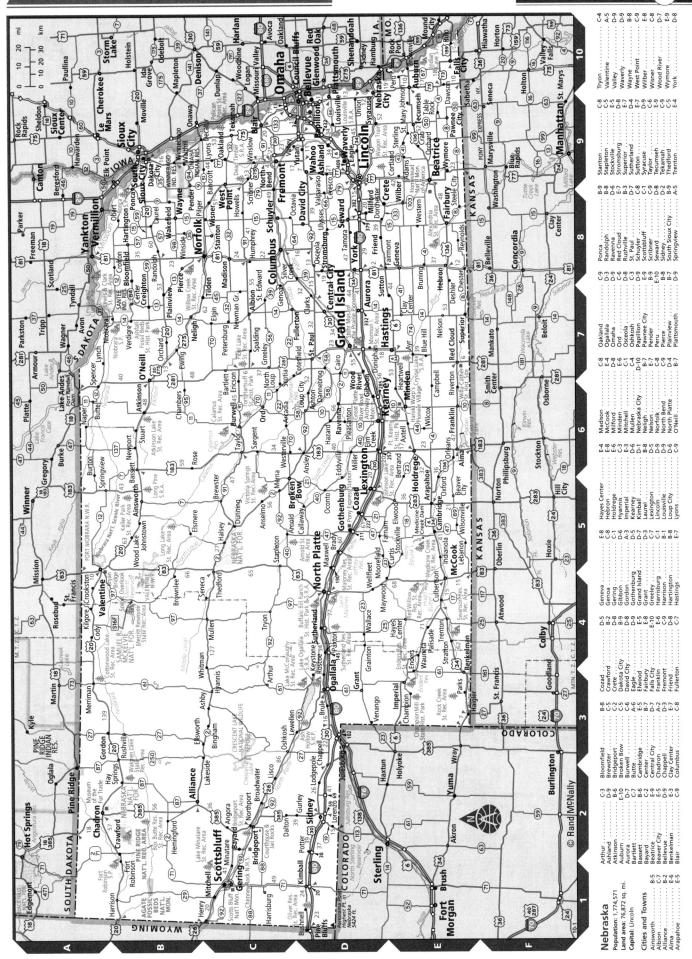

Nevada

Population: 2,565,382
Land area: 109,826 sq. mi.
Capital: Carson City

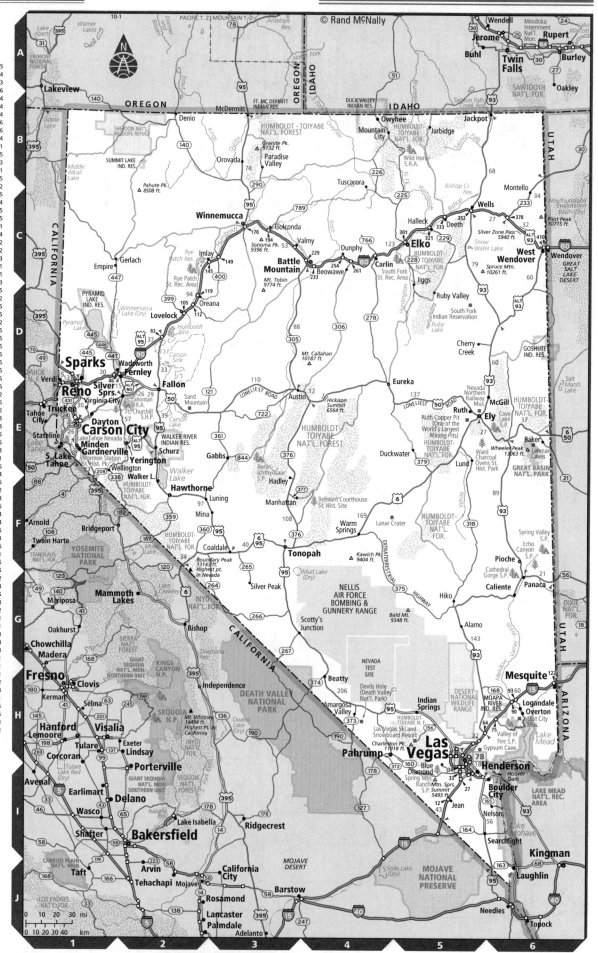

For border crossing information, please see p. 59

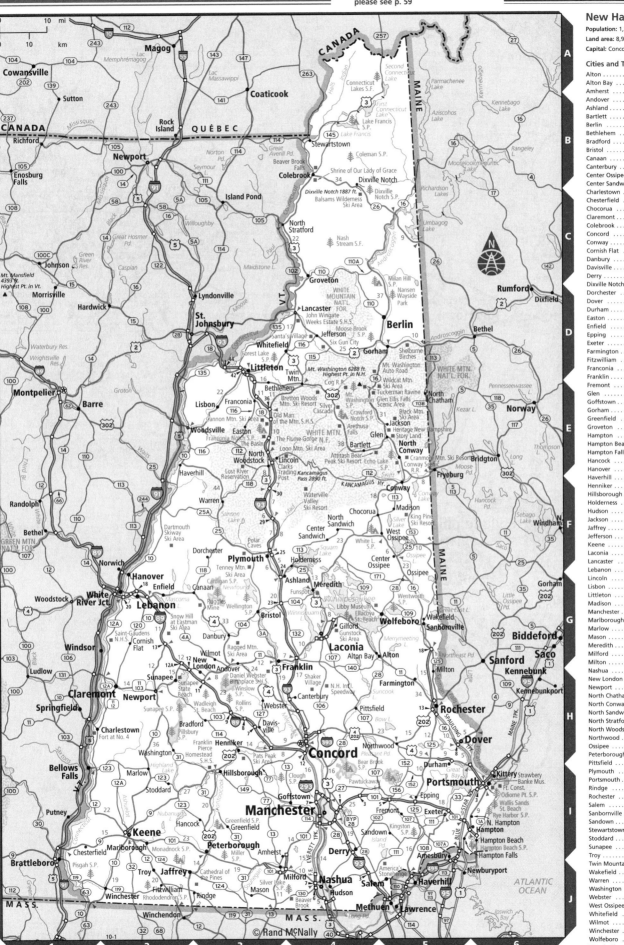

New Hampshire

Population: 1,315,828
Land area: 8,968 sq. mi.
Capital: Concord

Cities and Towns

New Jersey

Population: 8,685,920
Land area: 7,417 sq. mi.
Capital: Trenton

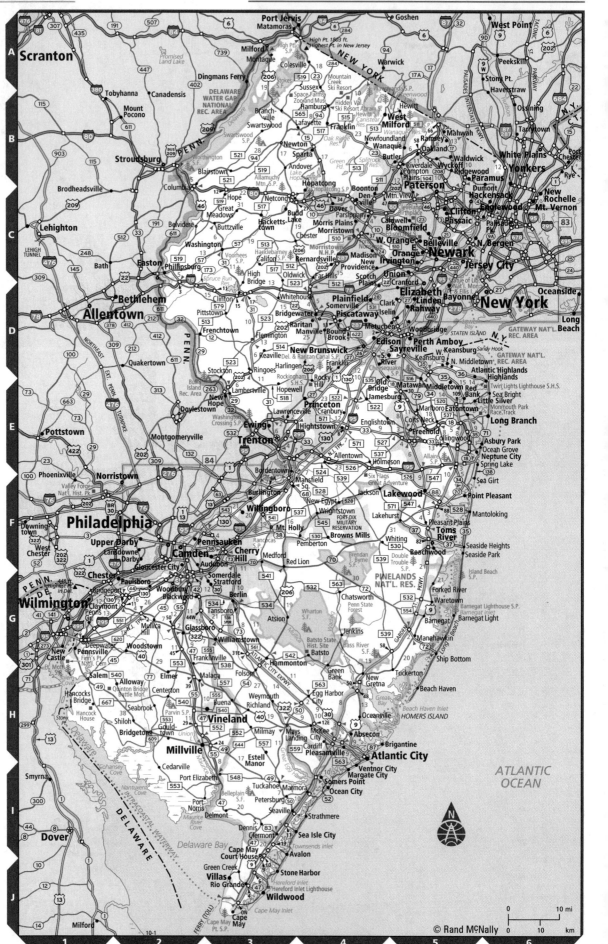

© Rand McNally

0   10 mi
0   10 km

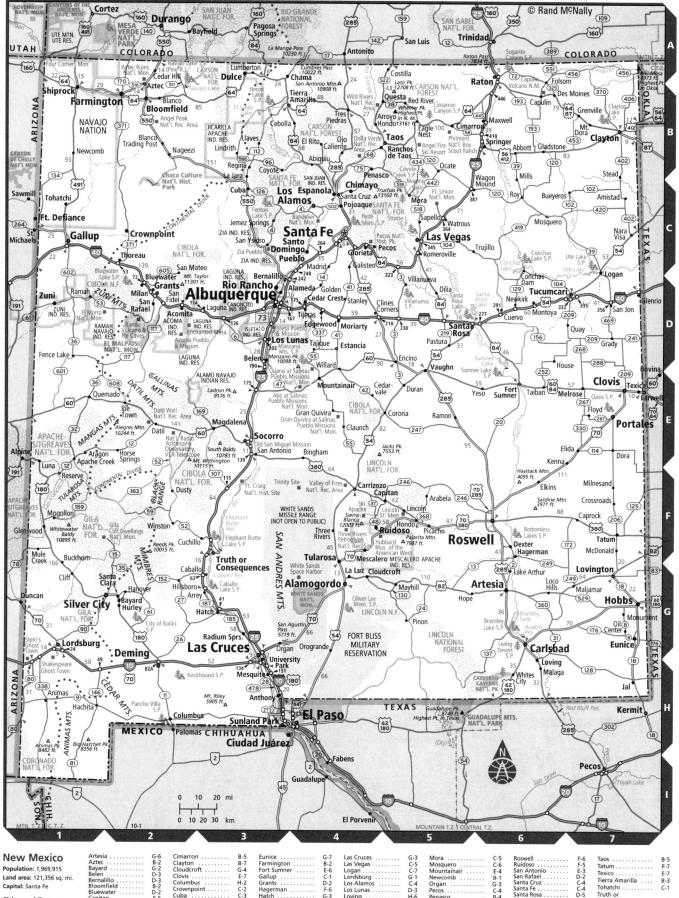

© Rand McNally

New Mexico

Population: 1,969,915
Land area: 121,356 sq. mi.
Capital: Santa Fe

Cities and Towns

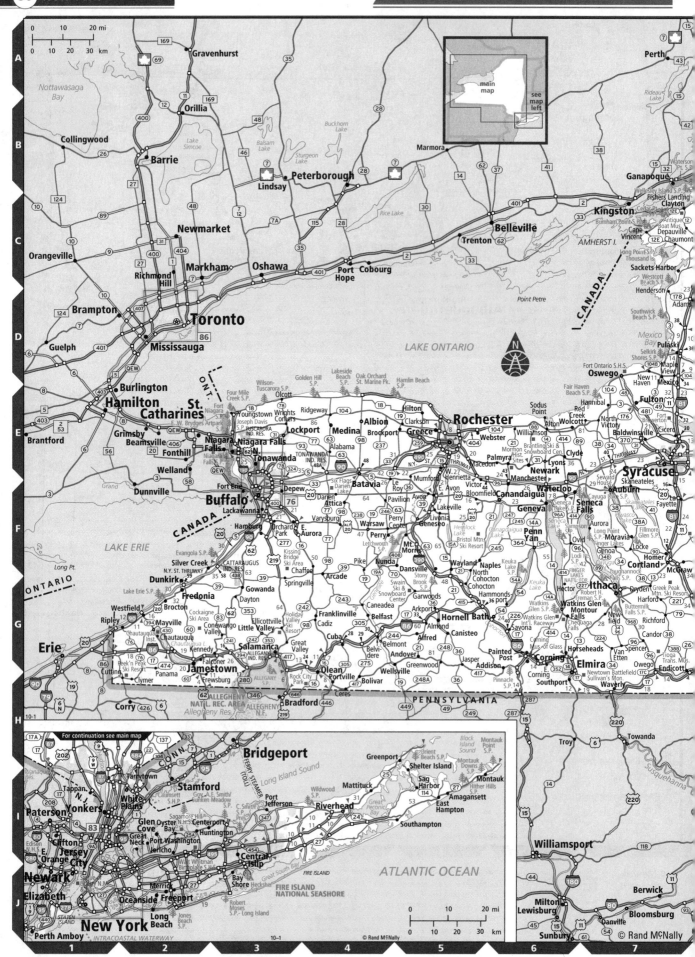

© Rand McNally

For border crossing information, please see p. 59

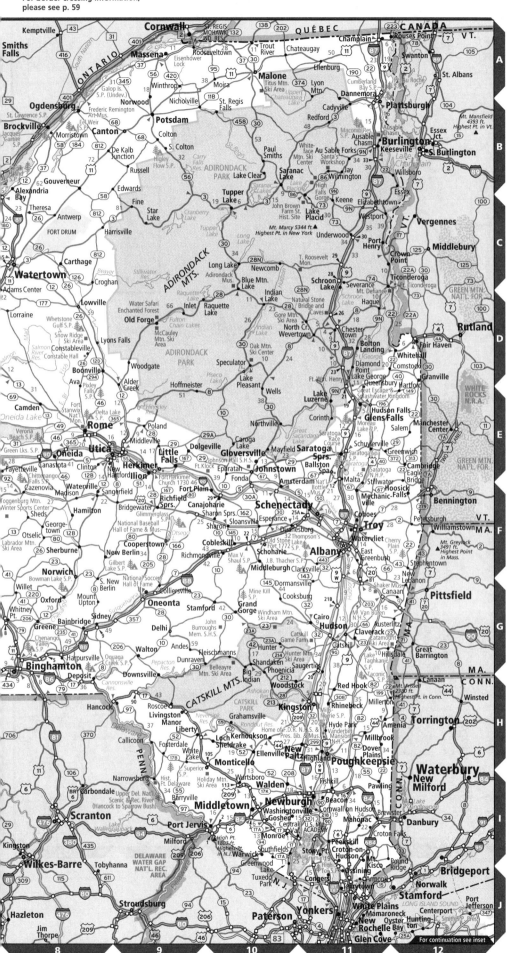

New York

Population: 19,297,729
Land area: 47,214 sq. mi.
Capital: Albany

Cities and Towns

Adams	D-7
Adams Center	D-8
Addison	G-6
Albany	F-11
Albion	E-4
Alexandria Bay	B-8
Alfred	G-5
Amagansett	I-11
Amenia	H-11
Amsterdam	F-10
Andover	G-5
Antwerp	C-8
Arcade	F-4
Attica	F-4
Au Sable Forks	B-11
Auburn	F-7
Avon	F-5
Bainbridge	G-8
Baldwinsville	E-7
Ballston Spa	E-11
Batavia	E-4
Bath	G-6
Bay Shore	J-3
Beacon	I-11
Belfast	G-4
Belmont	G-4
Binghamton	G-8
Blue Mountain Lake	C-10
Bolivar	H-4
Bolton Landing	D-11
Boonville	D-8
Brewster	I-11
Brockport	E-5
Brocton	G-2
Buffalo	F-3
Cadyville	G-11
Cairo	G-11
Cambridge	E-12
Camden	E-8
Canajoharie	F-10
Canandaigua	F-6
Canastota	E-8
Candor	G-7
Canisteo	G-5
Canton	B-9
Cape Vincent	C-7
Carthage	C-8
Catskill	G-11
Cazenovia	F-8
Centerport	J-2
Central Islip	I-3
Central Valley	I-10
Champlain	A-11
Chateaugay	A-10
Chaumont	C-7
Chautauqua	G-2
Cicero	E-7
Claverack	G-11
Clayton	C-7
Clinton	E-8
Clyde	E-6
Cobleskill	F-10
Cohocton	G-5
Cohoes	F-11
Congers	J-11
Cooperstown	F-9
Corinth	E-11
Corning	G-6
Cornwall on Hudson	I-11
Cortland	F-7
Croton Falls	I-11
Croton-on-Hudson	I-11
Crown Point	C-11
Cuba	G-4
Dannemora	B-11
Dansville	F-5
Delhi	G-9
Depew	F-3
Deposit	H-8
Dolgeville	E-9
Dover Plains	H-11
Downsville	H-9
Dryden	G-7
Dunkirk	F-2
East Aurora	F-3
East Greenbush	F-11
East Hampton	I-5
Elizabethtown	C-11
Ellenville	H-10
Elmira	H-6
Endicott	G-7
Falconer	G-2
Fayetteville	E-8
Fishkill	I-11
Fonda	F-10
Fort Plain	F-10
Franklinville	G-4
Fredonia	G-2
Freeport	J-2
Frewsburg	H-2
Fulton	E-7
Geneseo	F-5
Geneva	F-6
Glen Cove	J-11
Glens Falls	E-11
Gloversville	E-10
Goshen	I-10
Gouverneur	B-8
Gowanda	G-3
Grand Gorge	G-10
Granville	D-12
Great Neck	I-2
Greene	G-8
Greenport	H-5
Greenwich	E-11
Greenwood Lake	I-0
Hamburg	F-3
Hamilton	F-8
Hammondsport	G-6
Hancock	H-9
Herkimer	E-9
Highland	H-11
Hilton	E-5
Homer	F-7
Hoosick Falls	F-12
Hornell	G-5
Horseheads	H-6
Hudson	G-11
Hudson Falls	E-11
Huntington	J-12
Hyde Park	H-11
Ilion	E-9
Ithaca	G-7
Jamestown	G-2
Jericho	I-2
Johnstown	E-10
Keeseville	B-11
Kerhonkson	H-10
Kingston	H-11
Lackawanna	F-3
Lake George	D-11
Lake Luzerne	E-11

Lake Placid	C-11
Lake Pleasant	D-10
Lakeville	F-5
Le Roy	E-4
Liberty	H-9
Little Falls	E-9
Little Valley	G-3
Livingston Manor	H-9
Livonia	F-5
Loch Sheldrake	H-10
Lockport	E-3
Long Beach	J-2
Lowville	D-8
Lyon Mountain	A-11
Lyons	E-6
Macedon	E-6
Mahopac	I-11
Malone	A-10
Mamaroneck	J-11
Manchester	F-6
Massena	A-9
Mattituck	I-4
Mayfield	E-10
Mayville	G-2
Mechanicville	F-11
Medina	E-4
Merrick	J-2
Mexico	D-7
Middleburgh	F-10
Middletown	I-10
Millbrook	H-11
Millerton	H-11
Monroe	I-10
Montauk	I-6
Monticello	H-10
Montour Falls	G-6
Moravia	F-7
Mount Kisco	I-11
Mount Morris	F-5
Naples	F-5
New Berlin	F-9
New Hartford	E-8
New Paltz	H-11
New Rochelle	J-11
New York	J-1
Newark	E-6
Newburgh	I-11
Niagara Falls	E-3
North Tonawanda	E-3
Northville	E-10
Norwich	F-8
Norwood	A-9
Nunda	F-5
Oceanside	J-2
Ogdensburg	B-8
Olcott	E-3
Old Forge	D-9
Olean	H-4
Oneida	E-8
Oneonta	G-9
Orchard Park	F-3
Ossining	J-11
Oswego	D-7
Owego	G-7
Oxford	G-8
Oyster Bay	J-12
Painted Post	G-6
Palmyra	E-6
Paul Smiths	B-10
Pawling	I-11
Peekskill	I-11
Penn Yan	F-6
Perry	F-4
Plattsburgh	B-11
Port Henry	C-11
Port Jefferson	J-12
Port Jervis	I-10
Port Washington	I-2
Portville	H-4
Potsdam	B-9
Poughkeepsie	H-11
Pulaski	D-7
Red Hook	H-11
Rhinebeck	H-11
Richfield Springs	F-9
Ripley	G-2
Riverhead	I-4
Rochester	E-5
Rome	E-8
Roscoe	H-9
Rouses Point	A-12
Sackets Harbor	C-7
Sag Harbor	I-5
St. Regis Falls	B-10
Salamanca	G-3
Salem	E-12
Saranac Lake	B-10
Saratoga Springs	E-11
Saugerties	G-11
Schenectady	F-11
Schoharie	F-10
Schroon Lake	C-11
Schuylerville	E-11
Seneca Falls	F-6
Shelter Island	I-5
Sherburne	F-8
Sidney	G-8
Silver Creek	F-2
Skaneateles	F-7
Sodus Point	E-6
Southampton	I-5
Southport	H-6
Springville	G-3
Stamford	G-10
Star Lake	C-9
Stillwater	F-11
Stony Point	I-11
Syracuse	E-7
Tarrytown	J-11
Theresa	C-8
Ticonderoga	C-11
Troy	F-11
Tupper Lake	C-10
Utica	E-9
Victor	E-5
Walden	I-10
Walton	G-9
Warsaw	F-4
Warwick	I-10
Washingtonville	I-10
Waterloo	F-6
Watertown	C-8
Waterville	F-8
Watervliet	F-11
Watkins Glen	G-6
Waverly	H-7
Wayland	F-5
Webster	E-5
Wellsville	G-4
Westfield	G-2
White Plains	J-11
Whitehall	D-12
Whitney Point	G-8
Williamson	E-6
Wolcott	E-6
Woodstock	H-10
Wurtsboro	I-10
Yonkers	J-11
Youngstown	E-3

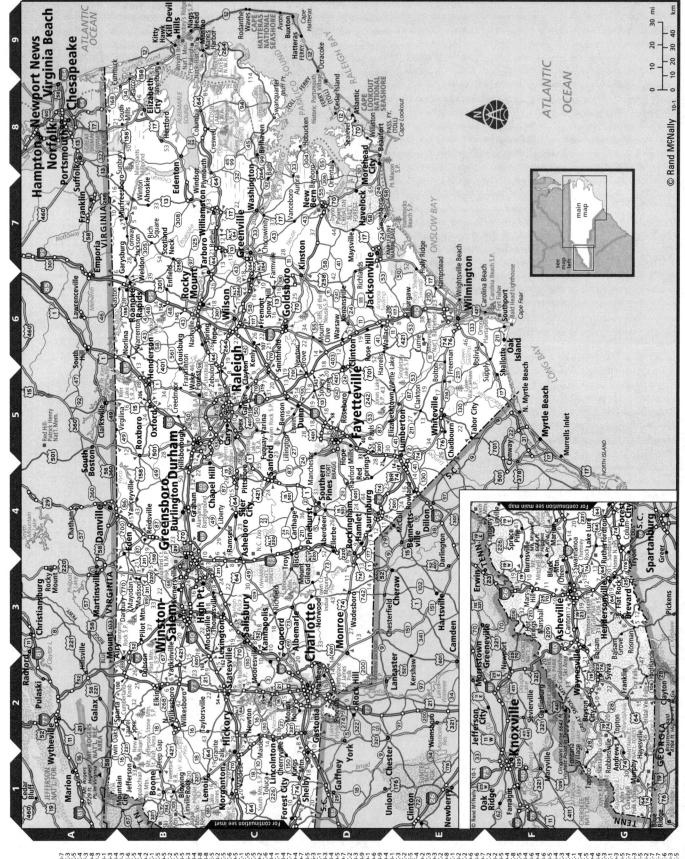

© Rand McNally

North Carolina

Population: 9,061,032
Land area: 48,711 sq. mi.
Capital: Raleigh

Cities and Towns

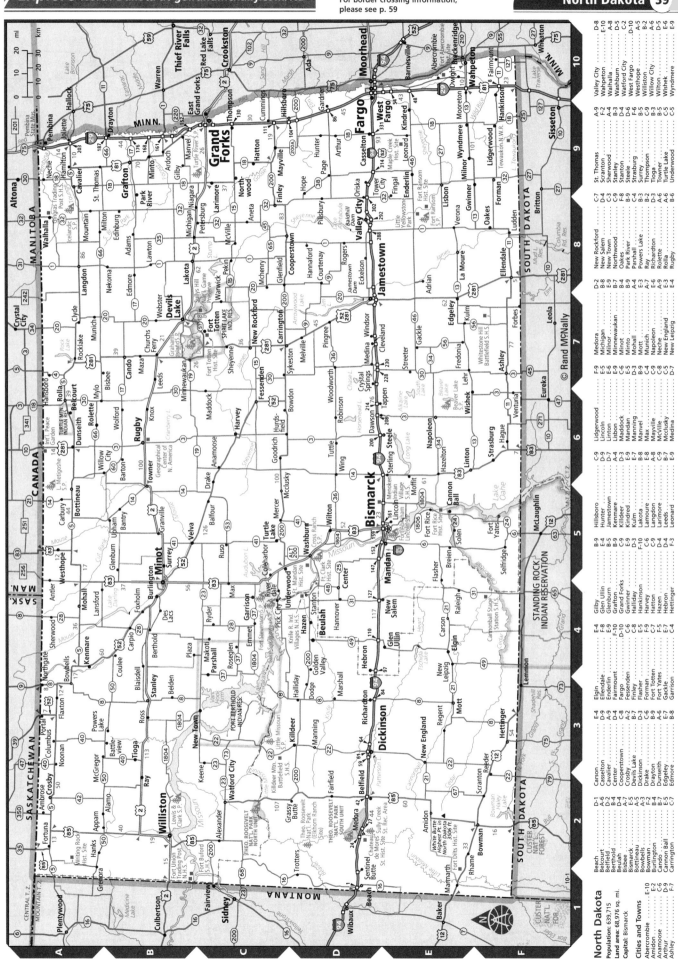

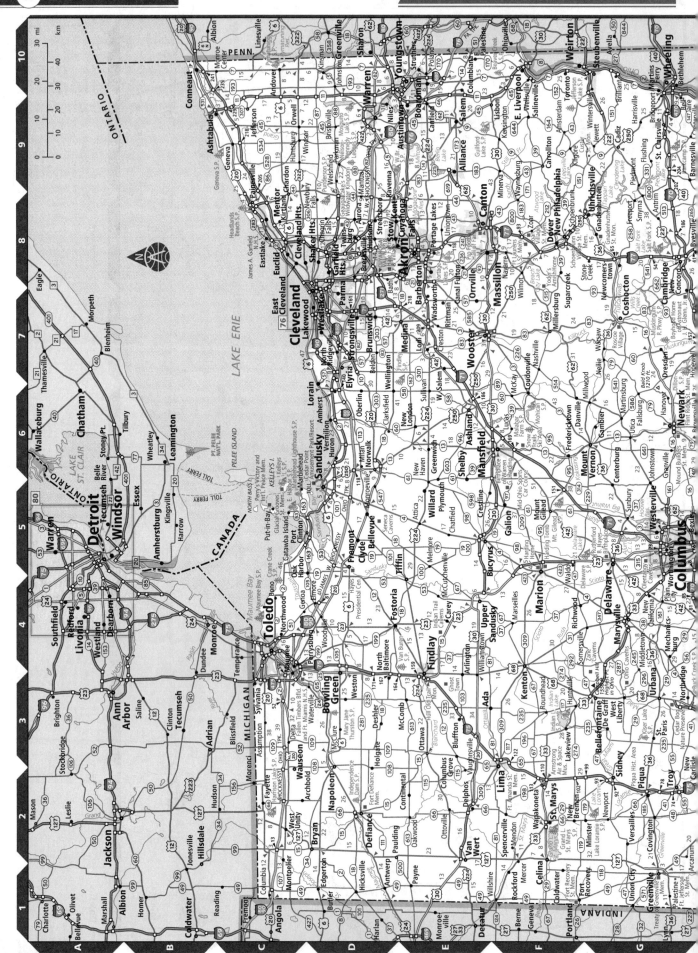

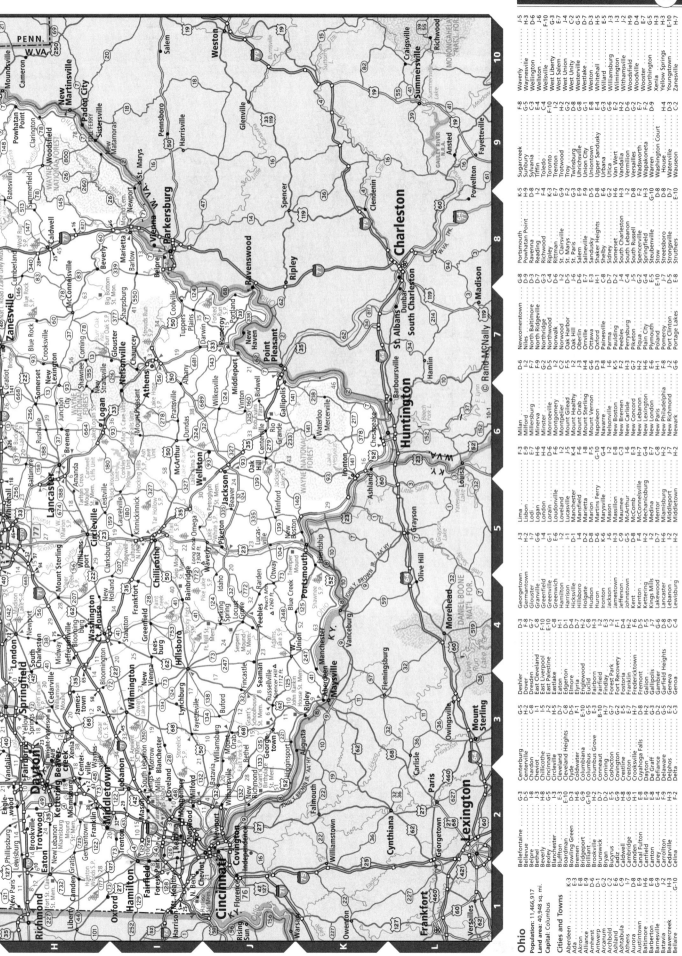

Ohio

Population: 11,466,917
Land area: 40,948 sq. mi.
Capital: Columbus

Cities and Towns

Aberdeen	K-3
Ada	E-8
Akron	D-6
Alliance	D-6
Amherst	D-9
Antwerp	G-10
Arcanum	G-9
Ashland	D-1
Ashtabula	C-9
Athens	G-6
Aurora	D-8
Austintown	D-9
Baltimore	H-6
Barberton	D-6
Barnesville	G-8
Batavia	J-2
Beavercreek	G-10
Bellaire	
Bellefontaine	G-3
Bellevue	I-8
Belpre	J-3
Bethel	H-8
Beverly	G-5
Bexley	E-3
Blanchester	E-3
Bluffton	D-8
Boardman	D-3
Bowling Green	H-6
Bremen	G-9
Bridgeport	G-10
Brookville	D-7
Brunswick	D-1
Bryan	D-2
Bucyrus	E-5
Cadiz	C-9
Caldwell	I-7
Cambridge	D-8
Canal Fulton	E-9
Canfield	H-6
Carey	E-9
Carrollton	J-2
Cedarville	H-3
Celina	G-10
Centerburg	G-3
Chardon	I-8
Cheviot	J-3
Chillicothe	H-8
Cincinnati	G-5
Circleville	E-3
Cleveland	E-8
Cleveland Heights	E-10
Clyde	D-3
Coldwater	H-6
Columbiana	G-9
Columbus Grove	G-10
Conneaut	D-7
Corning	E-5
Coshocton	D-8
Crestline	G-8
Creston	E-4
Cuyahoga Falls	E-8
Dayton	H-1
Defiance	D-8
Delaware	F-9
Delphos	H-3
Delta	F-2
Deshler	G-5
Dresden	H-2
East Cleveland	I-1
East Liverpool	I-5
East Palestine	E-6
Eastlake	H-5
Edgerton	D-7
Elmore	D-4
Elyria	F-1
Englewood	E-10
Fairborn	E-3
Fairfield	B-10
Fairport	H-7
Findlay	G-7
Forest Park	E-7
Fort Recovery	H-4
Franklin	H-7
Fredericktown	D-8
Fremont	D-5
Galion	D-2
Gambier	H-5
Garfield Heights	G-5
Geneva	C-4
Genoa	F-2
Georgetown	D-3
Germantown	G-7
Glouster	C-8
Granville	F-10
Greenfield	H-4
Greenville	I-2
Greenwich	D-1
Hamilton	E-6
Hicksville	D-4
Hillsboro	H-3
Holgate	I-2
Hubbard	H-3
Hudson	I-2
Huron	H-7
Jackson	I-2
Jamestown	H-3
Jefferson	J-4
Johnstown	G-5
Kent	F-6
Kenton	D-5
Kettering	G-6
Lakewood	D-7
Lancaster	C-8
Lebanon	H-1
Lewisburg	I-2
Lima	J-3
Lisbon	I-7
Lodi	G-7
Logan	I-4
London	G-1
Lorain	E-6
Loudonville	I-8
Loveland	F-2
Lucasville	J-5
Manchester	K-4
Mansfield	I-8
Marietta	H-4
Marion	G-6
Martins Ferry	H-1
Marysville	I-8
Massillon	G-10
Maumee	H-3
McArthur	G-5
McComb	F-4
McConnelsville	H-2
Mechanicsburg	E-7
Mentor	D-7
Miamisburg	H-1
Middleport	I-2
Middletown	G-10
Milan	F-3
Milford	E-7
Millersburg	F-9
Minerva	H-4
Minster	G-5
Monroeville	D-2
Montgomery	I-2
Montpelier	F-6
Mount Gilead	F-5
Mount Healthy	K-4
Mount Orab	I-8
Mount Sterling	H-4
Mount Vernon	G-6
Napoleon	G-10
Navarre	D-8
New Boston	K-5
New Bremen	F-2
New Carlisle	C-3
New Concord	I-6
New Lebanon	H-7
New Lexington	E-7
New London	C-8
New Paris	H-2
New Philadelphia	F-8
New Richmond	I-2
Newark	G-6
Newcomerstown	D-6
North Baltimore	F-2
North Ridgeville	F-9
Northridge	D-5
Northwood	G-2
Norwalk	I-2
Norwood	D-6
Oak Harbor	D-4
Oberlin	H-2
Orrville	G-3
Ottawa	F-9
Oxford	D-5
Painesville	H-8
Paulding	G-4
Peebles	K-5
Perrysburg	F-2
Piketon	I-6
Piqua	H-7
Poland	E-7
Pomeroy	C-8
Port Clinton	F-2
Portage Lakes	G-6
Portsmouth	G-8
Powhatan Point	F-2
Ravenna	D-7
Reading	D-3
Richwood	G-3
Ripley	K-3
Rittman	E-7
St. Clairsville	E-9
St. Marys	F-2
St. Paris	E-9
Salem	D-6
Salineville	J-6
Sandusky	E-7
Shaker Heights	H-1
Shelby	E-7
Somerset	F-8
South Charleston	E-3
South Russell	D-2
Spencerville	C-4
Springfield	J-5
Steubenville	G-2
Stow	E-10
Streetsboro	D-8
Strongsville	D-5
Struthers	E-8
Sugarcreek	K-5
Sunbury	H-9
Sylvania	D-8
Tiffin	I-2
Toledo	F-4
Toronto	K-3
Trenton	E-7
Trotwood	F-2
Twinsburg	G-3
Uhrichsville	E-9
Union City	G-3
Uniontown	D-5
Upper Sandusky	D-8
Urbana	E-4
Van Wert	H-6
Vandalia	E-2
Vermilion	D-6
Versailles	H-3
Wadsworth	D-8
Wapakoneta	F-2
Washington Court House	D-9
Waterville	D-7
Wauseon	E-10
Waverly	J-5
Waynesville	H-3
Wellington	J-6
Wellston	F-10
Wellsville	G-3
West Liberty	E-7
West Salem	J-4
West Union	C-2
West Unity	D-8
Westerville	G-1
Westlake	E-4
Weston	H-5
Whitehall	E-3
Willard	J-3
Williamsburg	E-2
Wilmington	H-9
Wintersville	D-6
Woodsfield	G-2
Woodville	E-7
Wooster	G-2
Worthington	D-9
Xenia	H-3
Yellow Springs	E-10
Youngstown	D-3
Zanesville	C-2

© Rand McNally

Oklahoma

Population: 3,617,316
Land area: 68,667 sq. mi.
Capital: Oklahoma City

Cities and Towns

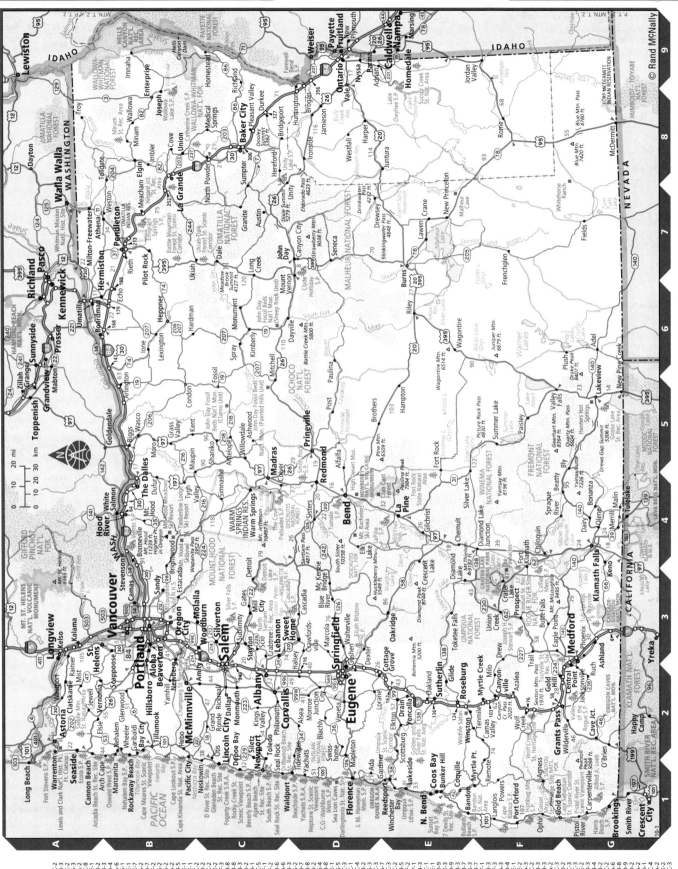

© Rand McNally

Oregon

Population: 3,747,455
Land area: 95,997 sq. mi.
Capital: Salem

Cities and Towns

Albany C-2
Aloha B-3
Amity C-2
Ashland G-3
Astoria A-2
Baker City C-8
Bandon E-1
Bay City B-2
Beaverton B-3
Bend D-4
Boardman A-6
Brookings G-1
Bunker Hill E-1
Burns D-7
Canby B-3
Cannon Beach A-2
Canyonville F-2
Cave Junction G-2
Central Point G-2
Clatskanie A-2
Condon B-5
Coos Bay E-1
Coquille E-1
Corvallis C-2
Cottage Grove D-2
Dallas C-2
Drain E-2
Eagle Point G-3
Elgin B-8
Enterprise B-8
Estacada B-3
Eugene D-2
Florence D-1
Fossil B-5
Gold Beach F-1
Grants Pass G-2
Heppner B-6
Hermiston A-6
Hillsboro B-3
Jacksonville G-2
John Day C-7
Joseph B-8
Junction City D-2
Klamath Falls G-4
La Grande B-8
Lakeside E-1
Lakeview G-5
Lebanon C-2
Lincoln City C-1
Madras C-4
McMinnville B-2
Medford G-3
Mill City C-3
Milton-Freewater A-7
Molalla B-3
Monmouth C-2
Moro B-5
Myrtle Creek F-2
Myrtle Point E-1
Newberg B-3
Newport C-1
North Bend E-1
Nyssa C-9
Oakridge D-3
Ontario C-9
Oregon City B-3
Pendleton B-7
Phoenix G-3
Pilot Rock B-7
Port Orford F-1
Portland B-3
Prospect F-3
Rainier A-3
Redmond D-4
Reedsport E-1
Roseburg E-2
St. Helens B-3
Salem C-2
Sandy B-3
Scappoose B-3
Seaside A-2
Silverton C-3
Springfield D-2
Stayton C-3
Sublimity C-3
Sutherlin E-2
Sweet Home D-3
The Dalles B-4
Tillamook B-2
Toledo C-1
Umatilla A-6
Union B-8
Vale C-9
Veneta D-2
Vernonia B-2
Waldport C-1
Warm Springs C-4
Warrenton A-2
Winston E-2
Woodburn C-3

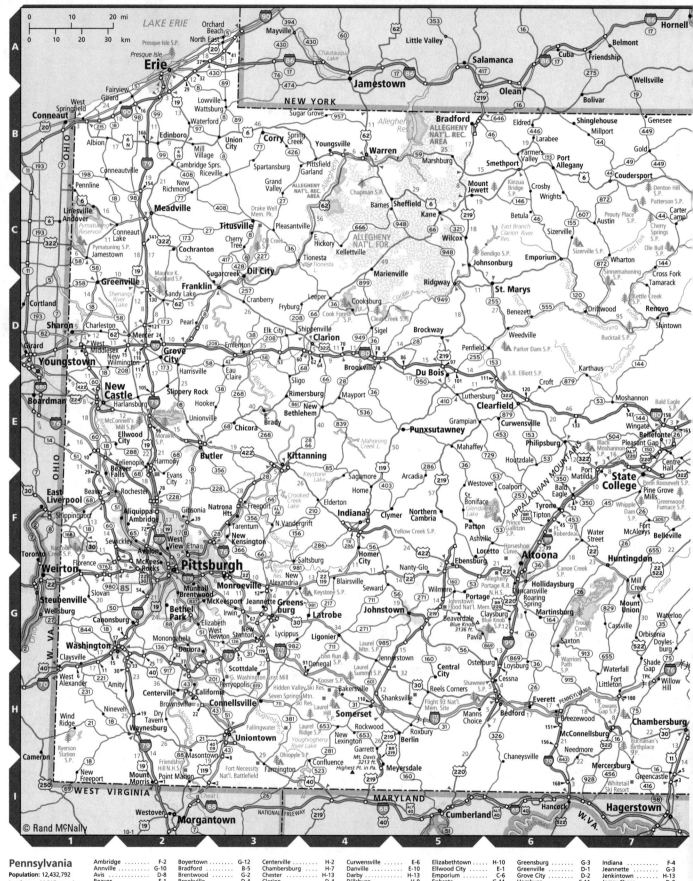

© Rand McNally

Pennsylvania

Population: 12,432,792
Land area: 44,817 sq. mi.
Capital: Harrisburg

Cities and Towns

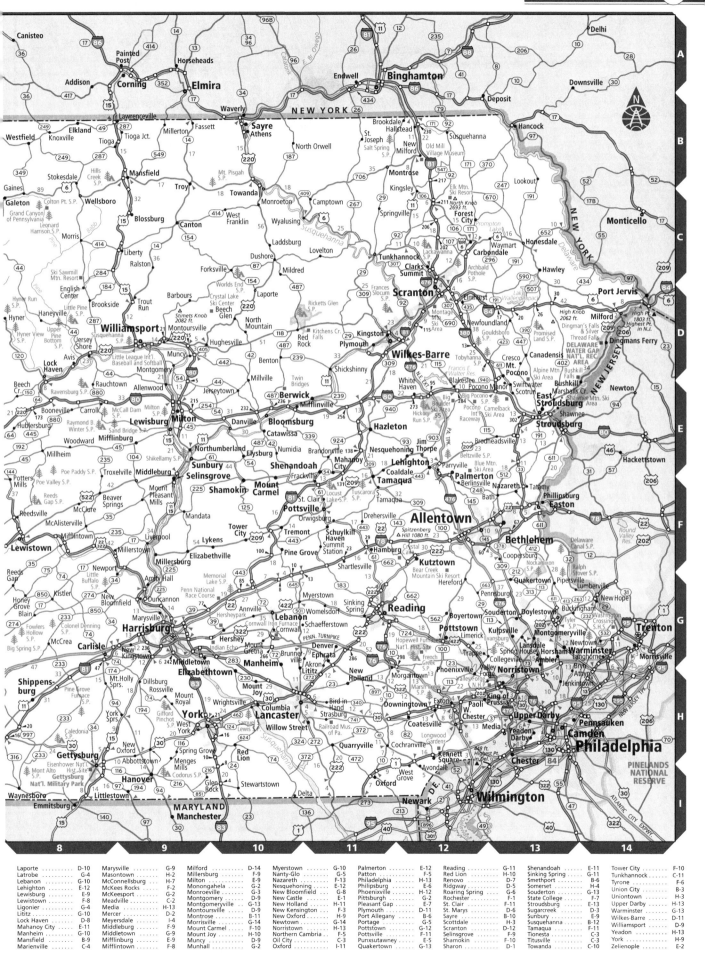

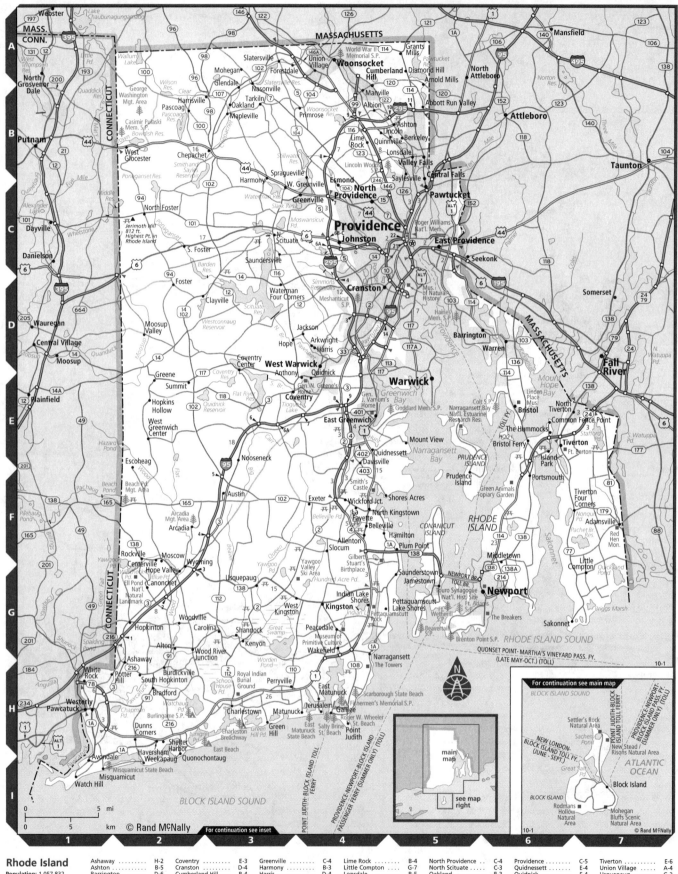

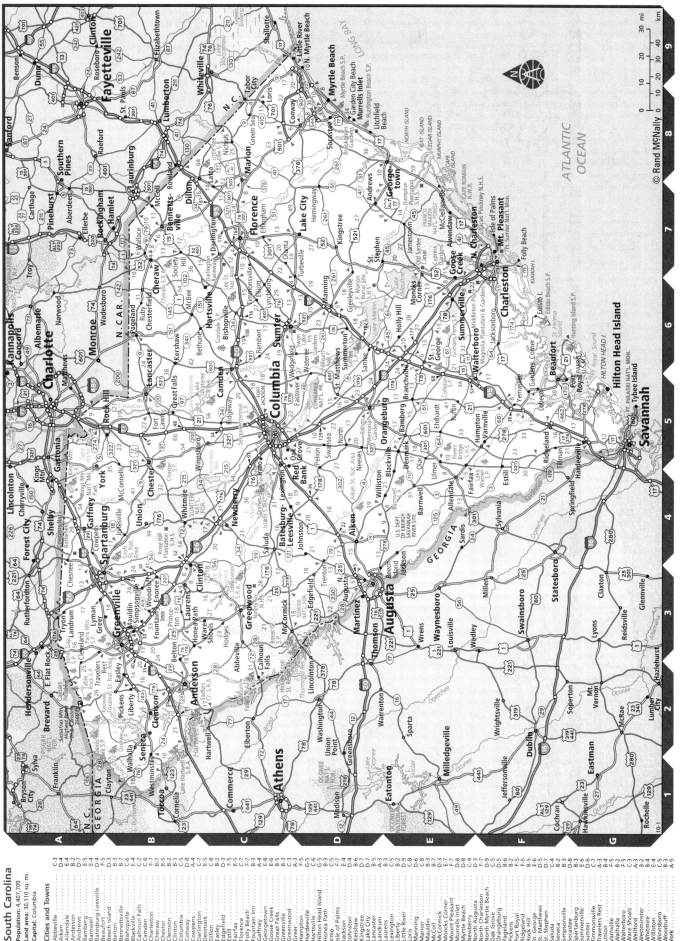

South Carolina

Population: 4,407,709
Land area: 30,110 sq. mi.
Capital: Columbia

Cities and Towns

South Dakota

Population: 796,214
Land area: 75,885 sq. mi.
Capital: Pierre

Cities and Towns

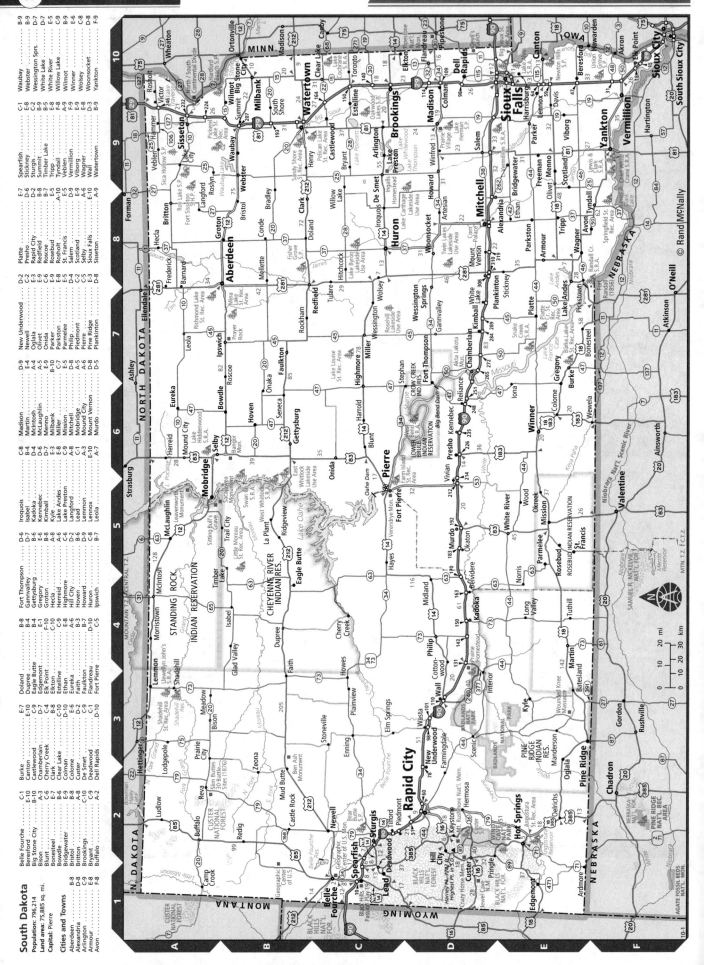

© Rand McNally

© Rand McNally

I-40 is scheduled to be completely closed between exits 388 and 389 in downtown Knoxville until late 2009. Visit www.tdot.state.tn.us/smartfix for more info.

Western Tennessee · Eastern Tennessee

Clingmans Dome 6643 ft. Highest Point in Tennessee

© Rand McNally

Tennessee

Population: 6,156,719
Land area: 41,217 sq. mi.
Capital: Nashville

Cities and Towns

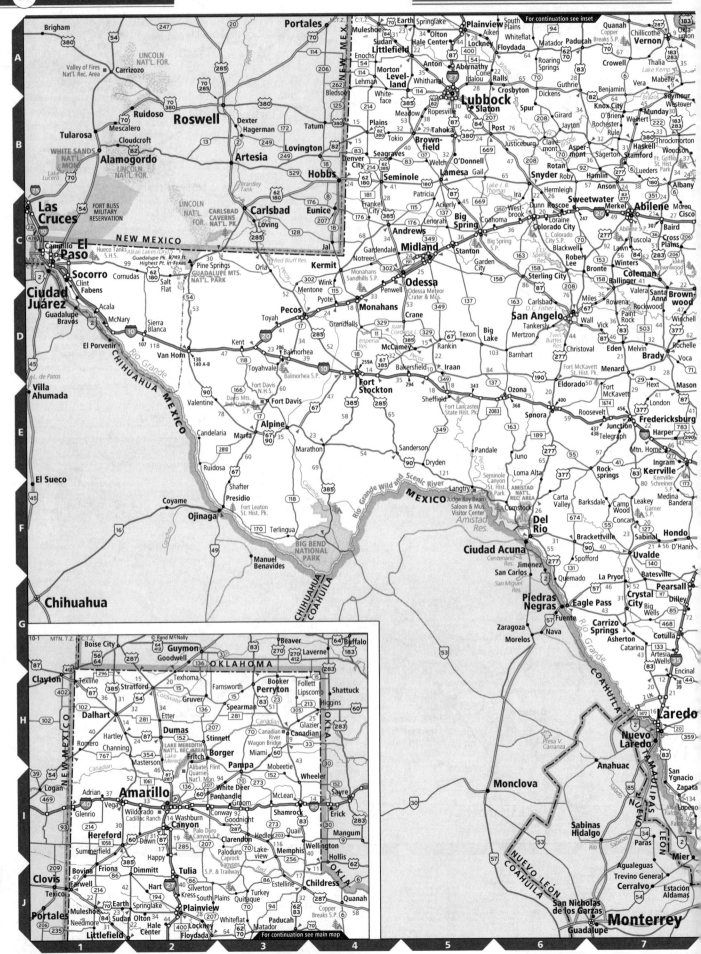

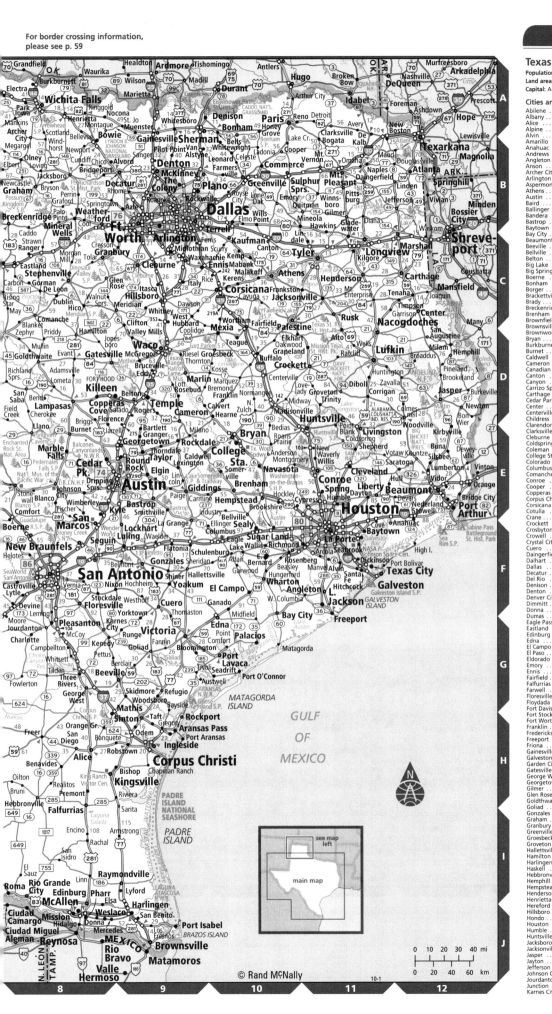

For border crossing information, please see p. 59

Texas

Population: 23,904,380
Land area: 261,797 sq. mi.

Capital: Austin

Cities and Towns

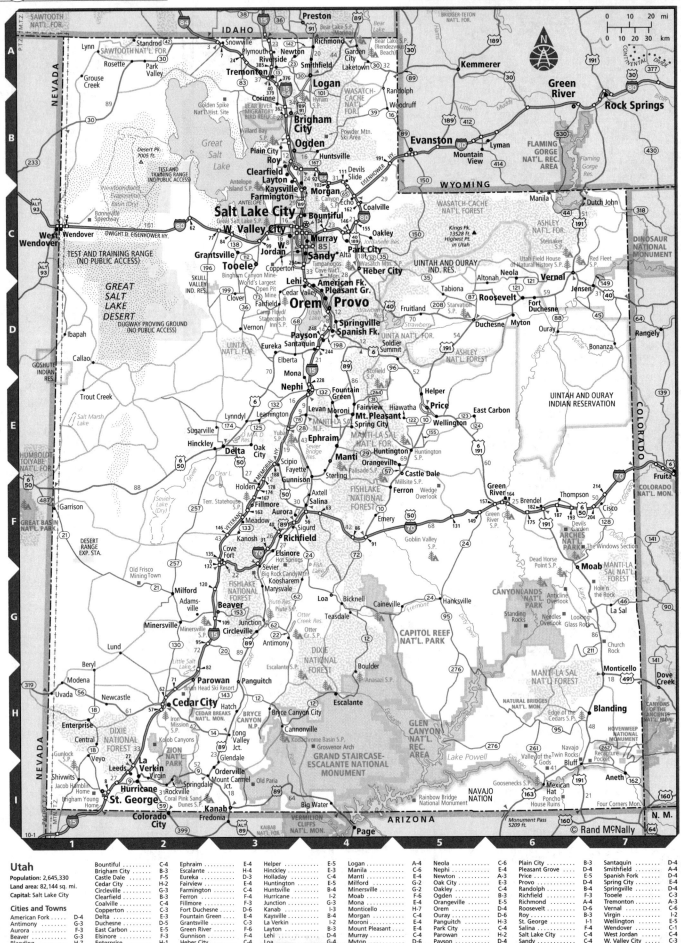

Utah

Population: 2,645,330
Land area: 82,144 sq. mi.
Capital: Salt Lake City

Cities and Towns

© Rand McNally

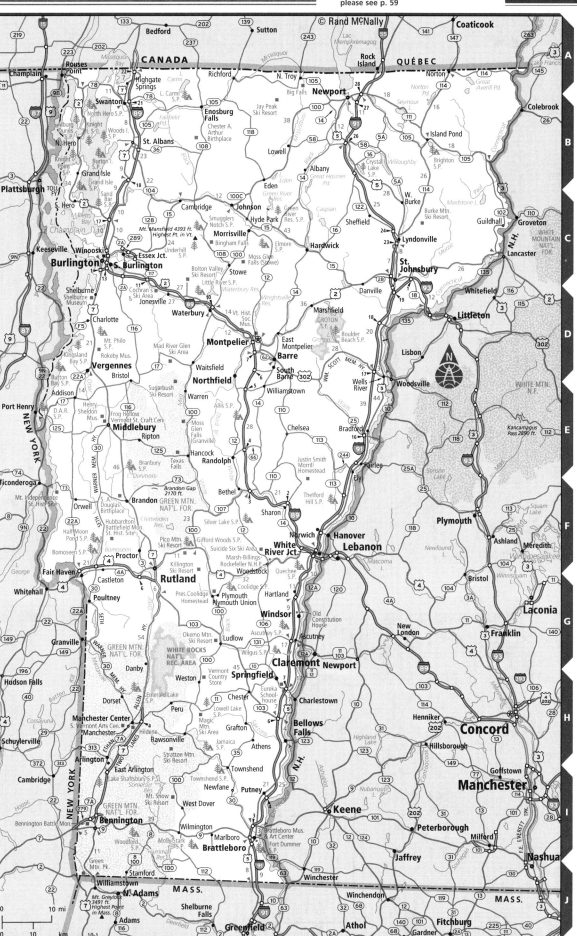

Vermont

Population: 621,254
Land area: 9,250 sq. mi.
Capital: Montpelier

Cities and Towns

Virginia

Population: 7,712,091
Land area: 39,594 sq. mi.
Capital: Richmond

Cities and Towns

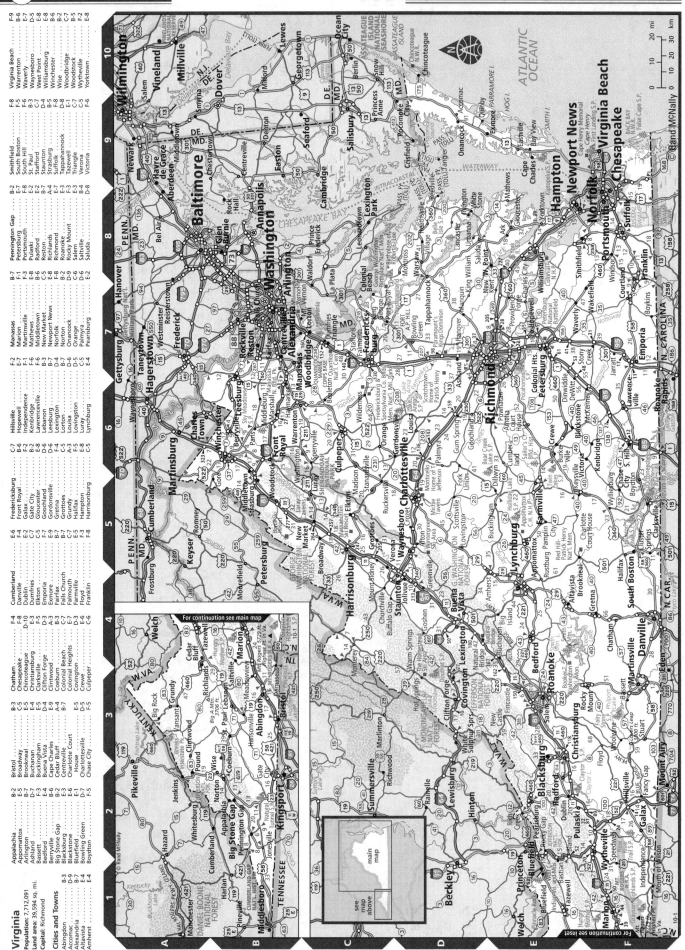

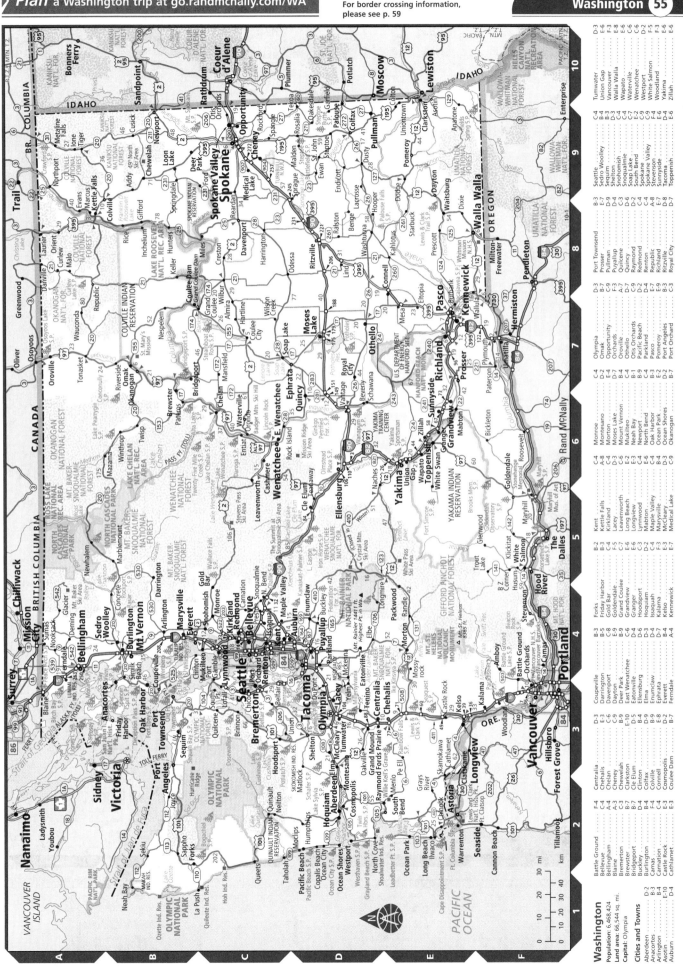

Washington

Population: 6,468,424
Land area: 66,544 sq. mi.
Capital: Olympia

West Virginia

Population: 1,812,035
Land area: 24,078 sq. mi.
Capital: Charleston

© Rand McNally

Wisconsin

Population: 5,601,640
Land area: 54,310 sq. mi.
Capital: Madison

Cities and Towns

Antigo	D-5	Beloit	H-5	Elkhorn	H-5	Kenosha	H-6	Menomonee Falls	G-6	Onalaska	F-2	River Falls	D-1	Washburn	B-3
Appleton	E-5	Berlin	F-5	Fond du Lac	F-5	Kewaunee	E-6	Menomonie	D-2	Oshkosh	F-5	Shawano	E-5	Watertown	G-5
Ashland	B-3	Black River Falls	E-3	Fort Atkinson	G-5	La Crosse	F-2	Mequon	G-6	Phillips	C-3	Sheboygan	F-6	Waukesha	G-6
Baraboo	G-4	Burlington	H-6	Grafton	G-6	Ladysmith	D-3	Merrill	D-4	Platteville	H-3	South Milwaukee	G-6	Waupaca	E-5
Beaver Dam	G-5	Chilton	E-6	Green Bay	E-6	Lake Geneva	H-6	Middleton	G-4	Plover	E-4	Sparta	F-3	Waupun	F-5
		Chippewa Falls	D-2	Hartford	G-6	Lancaster	H-3	Milwaukee	G-6	Plymouth	F-6	Stevens Point	E-4	Wausau	D-4
		Crandon	C-5	Hayward	C-2	Madison	G-4	Monroe	H-4	Port Washington	G-6	Stoughton	G-5	Wautoma	F-5
		Darlington	H-4	Hudson	D-1	Manitowoc	F-6	Mount Horeb	G-4	Portage	F-4	Sturgeon Bay	D-7	West Bend	G-6
		Delavan	H-5	Hurley	B-4	Marinette	D-6	Muskego	G-6	Prairie du Chien	G-3	Sun Prairie	G-5	Whitefish Bay	G-6
		De Pere	E-6	Janesville	H-5	Marshfield	E-4	Neenah	E-5	Racine	H-6	Superior	B-2	Whitewater	H-5
		Dodgeville	G-4	Jefferson	G-5	Mauston	F-4	New Glarus	H-4	Rhinelander	C-4	Tomah	F-3	Wisconsin Dells	F-4
		Eagle River	C-5	Juneau	G-5	Medford	D-3	Oconomowoc	G-5	Rice Lake	D-2	Tomahawk	D-4	Wisconsin Rapids	E-4
		Eau Claire	E-2	Kaukauna	E-6	Menasha	E-5	Oconto	D-6	Richland Cen.	G-3	Two Rivers	F-6	Viroqua	F-3

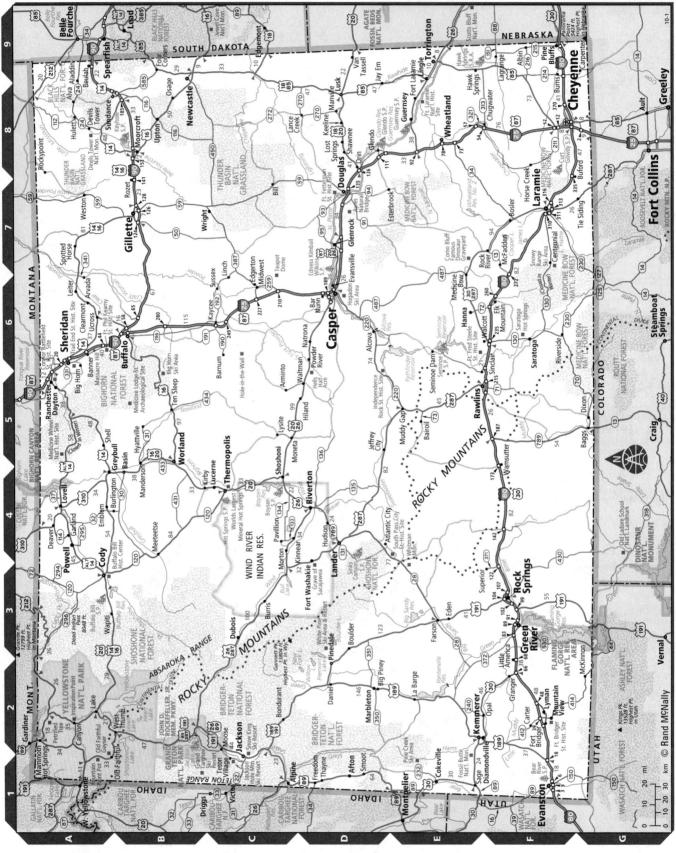

BORDER CROSSING INFORMATION

With advance planning, crossing the border to Mexico or Canada can be easier than you think.

Citizenship Documents

A U.S. passport or proof of citizenship, such as an original or certified birth certificate and photo identification is required for entry into Mexico or Canada. Naturalized U.S. citizens should carry citizenship papers; permanent residents of the United States must bring proof of residency and photo identification.

Traveling with Kids

For children under the age of 18, parents should be prepared to provide evidence, such as a birth certificate or adoption decree, to prove they are indeed the parents. Single or divorced parents and parents traveling without spouses should carry a letter of consent from the absent parent or guardian to bring a child across either border. Mexico requires the letter to be original and notarized. Divorced parents should also bring copies of their custody decree. Adults who are not the parents or guardians of the children they are traveling with must have written permission from the parents or guardians to supervise the children.

Minors traveling alone to Canada must have proof of citizenship and a letter from both parents detailing the length of stay, providing the parents' telephone number, and authorizing the person waiting for them to take care of them.

Re-entry to the U.S.

Proof of both citizenship and identity is required for entry into the United States.

The Western Hemisphere Travel Initiative (WHTI) is changing the requirements for re-entry into the U.S.

Since January 31, 2008, citizens of the United States, Canada, Mexico, and Bermuda traveling between the U.S. and Canada, Mexico, the Caribbean, and Bermuda by land or sea are required to present either a WHTI-compliant document (www.dhs.gov/xtrvlsec/crossingborders/#0), or a government-issued photo ID, such as a driver's license, plus proof of citizenship, such as a birth certificate, in order to re-enter the U.S. Children age 18 and under will be able to enter with proof of citizenship.

Beginning June 1, 2009, the U.S. government will implement the full requirements of the land and sea phase of WHTI. U.S. and Canadian citizens who are 16 years old and older traveling between the U.S. and Canada, Mexico, Central and South America, the Caribbean, and Bermuda by land or sea (including ferries), will be required to present a valid passport or other alternative documents as determined by the Department of Homeland Security (www.dhs.gov/xtrvlsec/crossingborders). U.S. and Canadian citizens who are 15 years old or younger will still be allowed to travel with only a copy of their birth certificate, as will teens ages 16-18 if they are part of an adult-supervised school, religious, cultural, or athletic group.

U.S. Passport Card

Since July 14, 2008, the U.S. passport card has been in production. The passport card facilitates entry and expedites document processing at U.S. land and sea ports-of-entry when arriving from Canada, Mexico, the Caribbean and Bermuda. The card may not be used to travel by air. Otherwise, it carries the rights and privileges of the U.S. passport book and is adjudicated to the exact same standards (www.travel.state.gov/passport/ppt_card/ppt_card_3926.html).

Mexico Only

Driving in Mexico

According to the U.S. Department of State, tourists traveling beyond the border zone must obtain a temporary import permit or risk having their car confiscated by Mexican customs officials. To acquire a permit, you must submit evidence of citizenship, title for the car, a car registration certificate, driver's license, and a processing fee to either a Banjercito (Mexican Army Bank) branch located at a Mexican Customs office at the port of entry, or at one of the Mexican consulates in the U.S. Mexican law also requires posting a bond at a Banjercito office to guarantee departure of the car from Mexico within a period determined at the time of application. In order to recover this bond or avoid credit card charges, travelers must go to any Mexican Customs office immediately prior to departing Mexico. Carry proof of car ownership (the current registration card or a letter of authorization from the finance or leasing company). Mexican law also requires that owners either drive their vehicles or be inside the vehicle when it is being driven. Auto insurance policies, other than Mexican, are not valid in Mexico. A short-term liability policy is obtainable at the border.

Tourist Cards

Tourist cards are valid up to six months, require a fee, and are required for all persons, regardless of age, who are traveling in Mexico outside the "border zone." Cards may be obtained from Mexican border authorities, Consuls of Mexico, or Federal Delegates in major cities. Cards are also distributed to passengers en route to Mexico by air.

Fast Pass for Frequent Travelers

For frequent travelers, it is possible to apply for a SENTRI card, which allows pre-screened, low-risk travelers to be processed with little or no delay at land border crossings. Approved applicants are issued an identification card and they can quickly cross the border in a dedicated traffic lane without routine customs and immigration questioning (unless they are randomly selected).

For additional information on traveling in Mexico, contact the Mexican Embassy in Washington, D.C.: (202) 736-1000; or visit http://portal.sre.gob.mx/usa/. You also can visit the U.S. Department of State Website, http://travel.state.gov/travel/cis_pa_tw/cis/cis_970.html.

Canada Only

Driving in Canada

Drivers need proof of ownership of the vehicle or documentation of its rental, a valid U.S. driver's license, and automobile insurance.

Fast Pass for Frequent Travelers

For frequent travelers, the United States and Canada have instituted the NEXUS program, which allows pre-screened, low-risk travelers to be processed with little or no delay by U.S. and Canadian border officials.

For additional information on traveling in Canada, contact the Canadian Embassy in Washington, D.C.: (202) 682-1740; www.canadianembassy.org or go to the U.S. Department of State Website, http://travel.state.gov/travel/cis_pa_tw/cis/cis_1082.html.

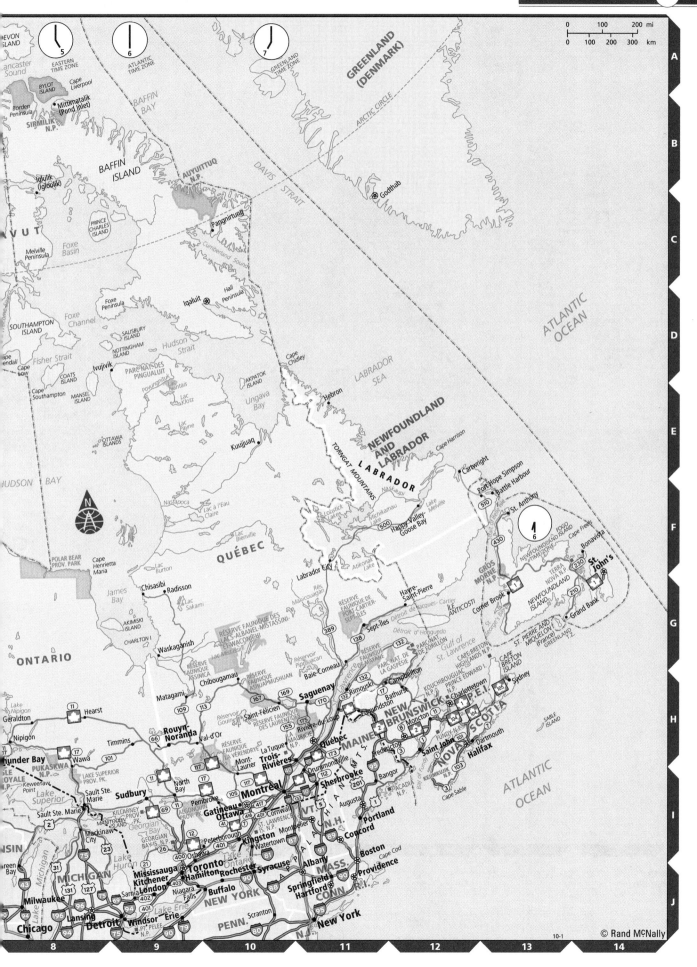

© Rand McNally

10-1

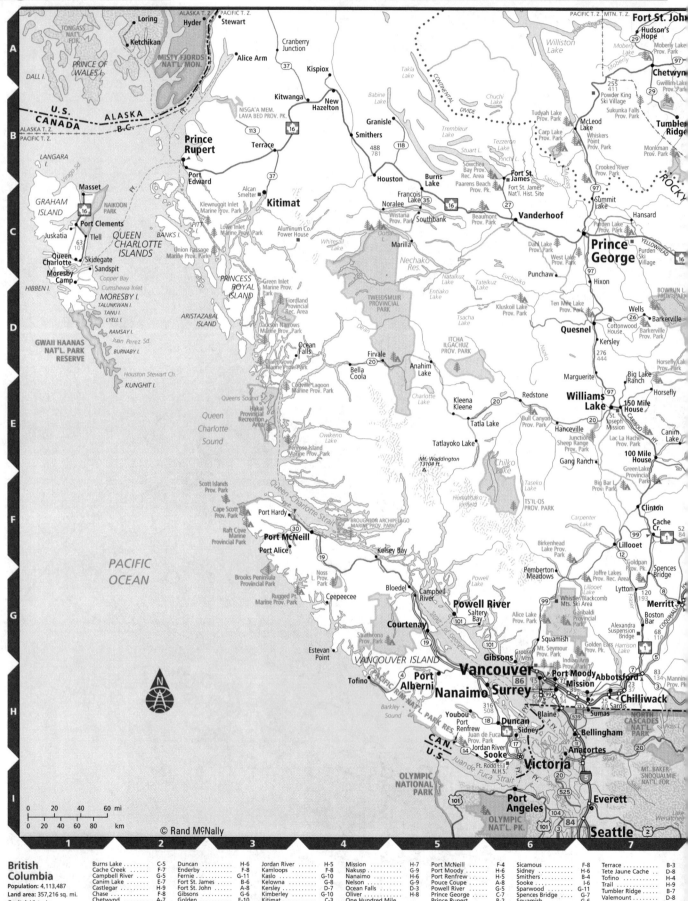

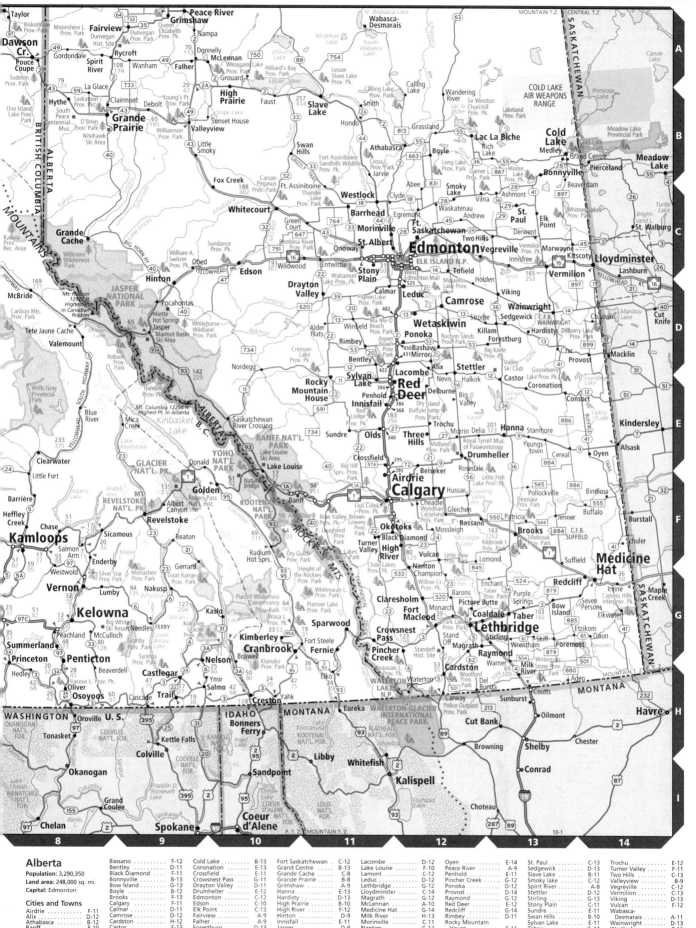

Alberta

Population: 3,290,350
Land area: 248,000 sq. mi.
Capital: Edmonton

Cities and Towns

Manitoba
Population: 1,148,401
Land area: 213,729 sq. mi.
Capital: Winnipeg

Cities and Towns

Saskatchewan
Population: 968,157
Land area: 228,445 sq. mi.
Capital: Regina

Cities and Towns

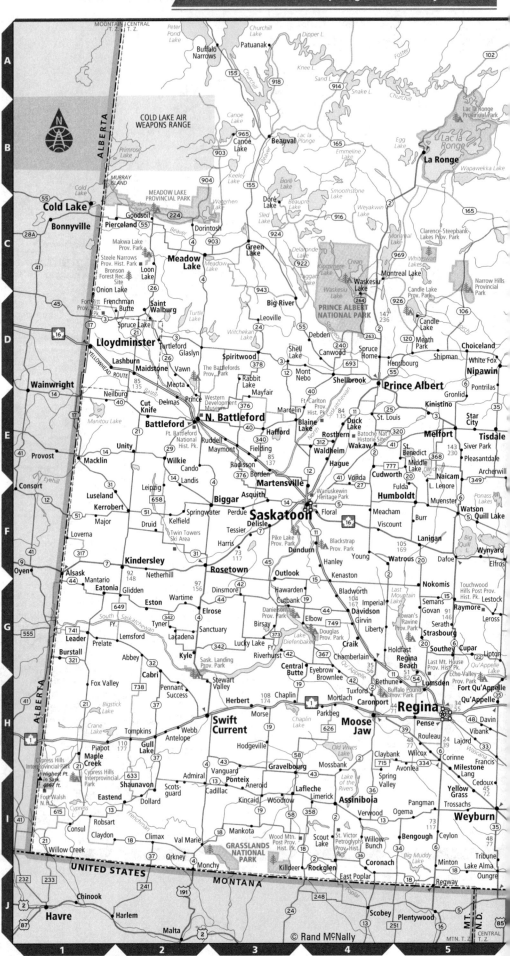

© Rand McNally

For border crossing information, please see p. 59

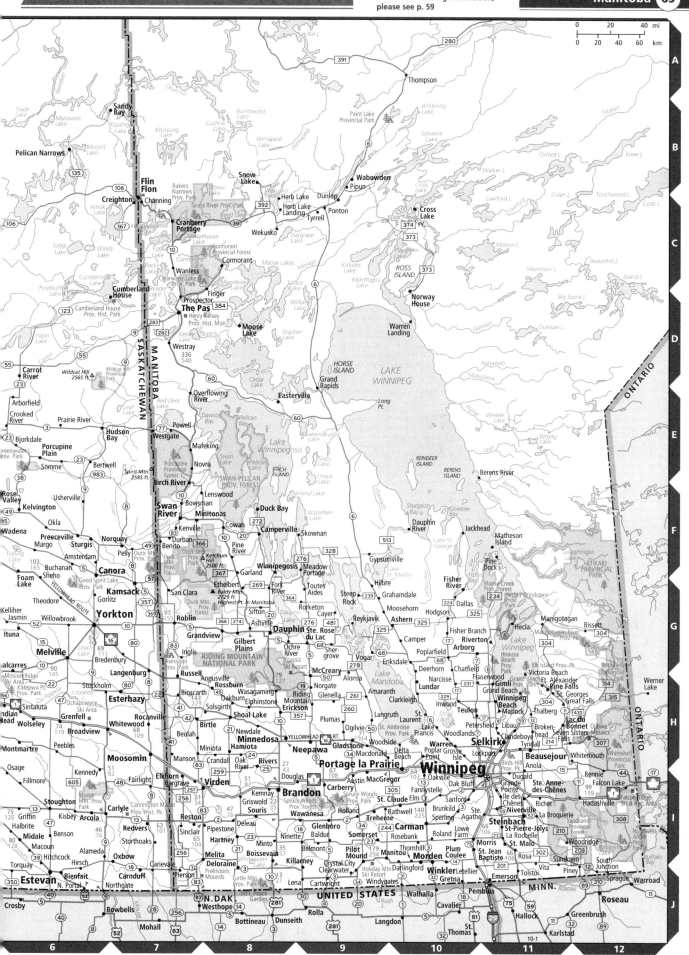

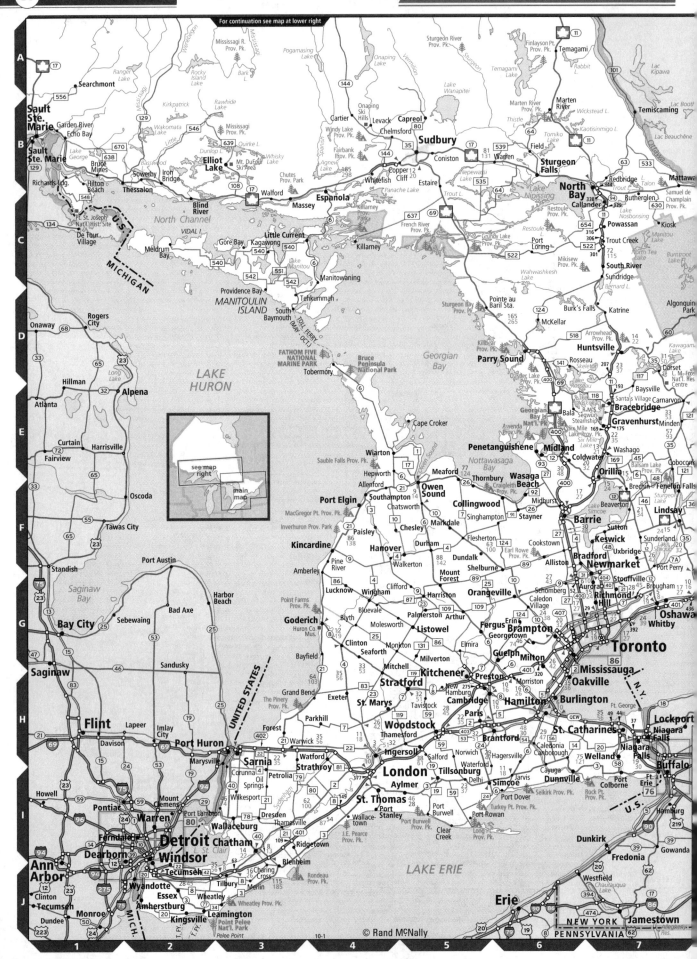

© Rand McNally

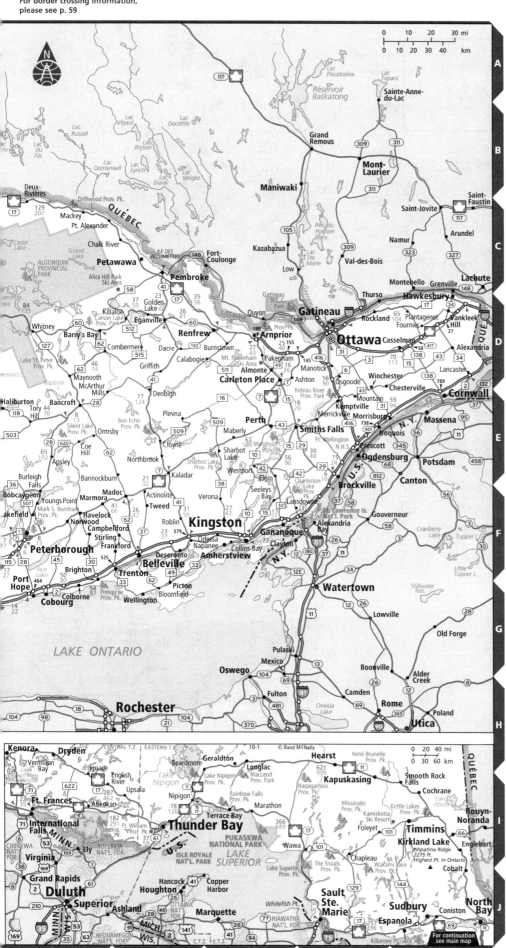

Ontario

Population: 12,160,282
Land area: 354,342 sq. mi.
Capital: Toronto

main map

see map right

Québec

Population: 7,546,131
Land area: 527,079 sq. mi.
Capital: Québec

Cities and Towns

For border crossing information, please see p. 59

© Rand McNally

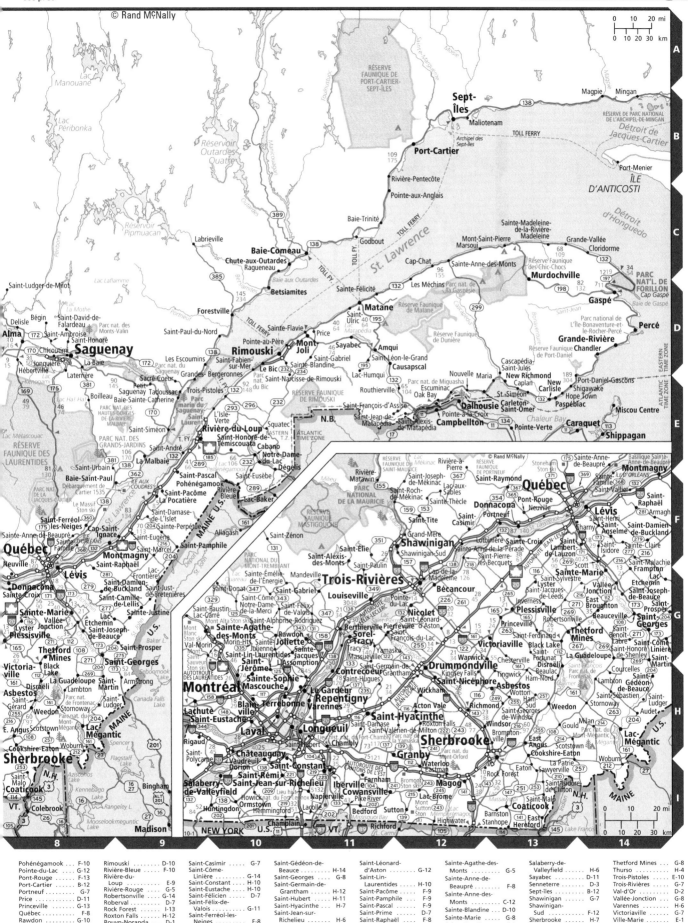

Get more Atlantic Provinces info at go.randmcnally.com/AP

New Brunswick

Population: 729,997
Land area: 27,587 sq. mi.
Capital: Fredericton

Cities and Towns

Acadie Siding	E-5
Adamsville	E-5
Alma	G-6
Anagance	F-5
Bathurst	C-5
Belledune	C-5
Big Cove	E-6
Blackville	E-5
Blissfield	E-5
Boiestown	E-4
Bouctouche	E-6
Campbellton	C-4
Canaan	F-6
Cap-Pele	F-6
Cape Tormentine	F-7
Caraquet	C-6
Chatham	D-5
Chipman	F-5
Coles Island	F-5
Cross Creek	F-4
Dalhousie	C-4
Doaktown	E-4
Eastport	H-4
Edmundston	D-2
Escuminac	D-6
Florenceville	E-3
Fredericton	F-4
Grand Falls (Grand Sault)	D-3
Hammondvale	G-5
Hampton	G-5
Harcourt	E-5
Hartland	F-3
Harvey	F-4
Hillsborough	F-6
Jemseg	F-5
Juniper	E-3
Kedgwick	C-3
Keswick Ridge	F-4
Kouchibouguac	C-6
Lameque	C-6
Lawrence Station	G-3
Long Creek	F-4
Lutes Mountain	F-6
Memramcook	F-6
Millville	F-3
Minto	F-5
Miramichi	D-5
Moncton	F-6
Nashwaak Bridge	F-4
Neguac	D-5
Newcastle	D-5
Nictau	D-3
North Head	H-4
Oromocto	F-4
Perth-Andover	E-3
Plaster Rock	E-3
Pointe-Sapin	E-6
Pointe-Verte	C-5
Port Elgin	F-6
Renous	E-5
Rexton	E-6
Richibucto	E-6
Riverside-Albert	F-6
Rogersville	E-5
Sackville	F-6
St. Andrews	G-3
St. Croix	G-3
St. George	G-4
Saint John	G-5
St. Martins	G-5
St-Quentin	D-3
St. Stephan	G-3
Salisbury	F-6
Shediac	F-6
Shippagan	C-6
Sussex	G-5
Sussex Corner	G-5
Thomaston Corner	G-3
Tracy	F-4
Upper Hainesville	F-3
Welsford	G-4
Woodstock	F-3
Youngs Cove	F-5

Newfoundland and Labrador

Population: 505,469
Land area: 144,353 sq. mi.
Capital: St. John's

Cities and Towns

Baie Verte	B-11
Bay de Verde	C-12
Bishop's Falls	C-11
Bonavista	C-12
Brig Bay	A-10
Buchans	C-10
Burgeo	C-10
Channel-Port aux Basques	C-9
Corner Brook	C-10
Daniel's Harbour	B-10
Deer Lake	C-10
Englee	B-11
Gander	C-11
Goobies	C-12
Grand Bank	D-11
Grand Falls-Windsor	C-11
Harbour Breton	D-11
Lark Harbour	C-10
Marystown	D-11
Placentia	D-12
Port Blandford	C-11
Roddickton	B-11
Rose-Blanche-Harbour le Cou	C-10
St. Alban's	C-11
St. Anthony	A-11
St. John's	C-12
St. Lawrence	D-11
Torbay	C-12
Trout River	B-10

Nova Scotia

Population: 913,462
Land area: 20,594 sq. mi.
Capital: Halifax

Cities and Towns

Advocate Harbour	G-6
Albany Cross	H-6
Amherst	F-6
Annapolis Royal	H-5
Antigonish	G-9
Apple River	G-6
Baddeck	F-10
Barrington Passage	J-5
Bass River	G-7
Big Pond	F-10
Bridgetown	H-5
Bridgewater	I-6
Brookfield	G-7
Brooklyn	H-7
Canso	G-10
Carleton	I-5
Centreville	H-5
Chester	H-6
Cheticamp	E-10
Clementsport	H-5
Clyde River	J-5
Corberrie	I-5
Dartmouth	H-7
Digby	H-5
East Bay	F-11
Earltown	G-7
Elmsdale	H-7
Glace Bay	F-11
Glenholme	G-7
Goldboro	G-9
Goldenville	G-9
Grand River	F-10
Greywood	H-5
Guysborough	G-9
Halifax	H-7
Halls Harbour	G-6
Hebron	I-5
Indian Brook	E-10
Ingonish	E-11
Ingonish Beach	E-10
Inverness	F-10
Joggins	G-6
Kentville	H-6
Larrys River	G-9
Liverpool	I-6
Lockeport	J-5
Louisbourg	F-11
Lunenburg	I-6
Maccan	F-6
Mahone Bay	I-6
Margaree Forks	E-10
Margaree Harbour	E-10
Mavillete	I-4
Middle Musquodoboit	H-7
Middlefield	I-6
Middleton	H-6
Mill Village	I-6
Moser River	H-8
Mulgrave	G-9
Musquodoboit Harbour	H-7
Neil's Harbour	E-11
New Germany	H-6
New Glasgow	G-8
New Ross	H-6
New Waterford	E-11
Newport Station	H-6
North Sydney	F-11
Nyanza	F-10
Oxford	F-7
Parrsboro	G-6
Peggys Cove	H-7
Picton	G-8
Pleasant Bay	E-10
Port Hastings	F-9
Port Hawkesbury	G-10
Port Hood	F-9
Pubnico	J-5
Sable River	I-6
St. Peters	G-10
Salmon River	I-5
Sand Point	G-10
Shag Harbour	J-5
Sheet Harbour	H-8
Shelburne	J-5
South Brookfield	I-6
Southampton	G-6
Springhill	G-6
Stewiacke	G-7
Sunnybrae	G-8
Sydney	F-11
Sydney Mines	E-11
Tatamagouche	G-7
Tiverton	I-4
Truro	G-7
Upper Musquodoboit	G-8
Upper Rawdon	H-7
Vaughan	H-6
Wedgeport	J-5
Westport	I-4
Weymouth	I-5
Whycocomagh	F-10
Windsor	H-6
Wolfville	G-6
Yarmouth	I-5

Prince Edward Island

Population: 135,851
Land area: 2,185 sq. mi.
Capital: Charlottetown

Cities and Towns

Alberton	E-6
Belle River	F-8
Borden-Carleton	F-7
Campbellton	E-6
Cavendish	E-7
Charlottetown	F-7
Georgetown	F-8
Kensington	E-7
Montague	F-8
Murray Harbour	F-8
Portage	E-6
Rocky Point	F-7
St. Peters	E-8
Souris	E-8
South Lake	E-9
Summerside	E-7
Tignish	D-6
West Point	E-6

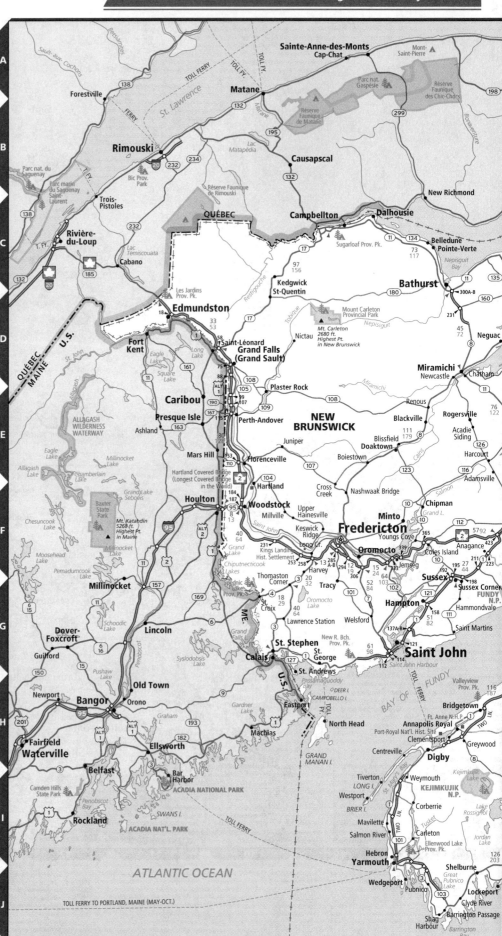

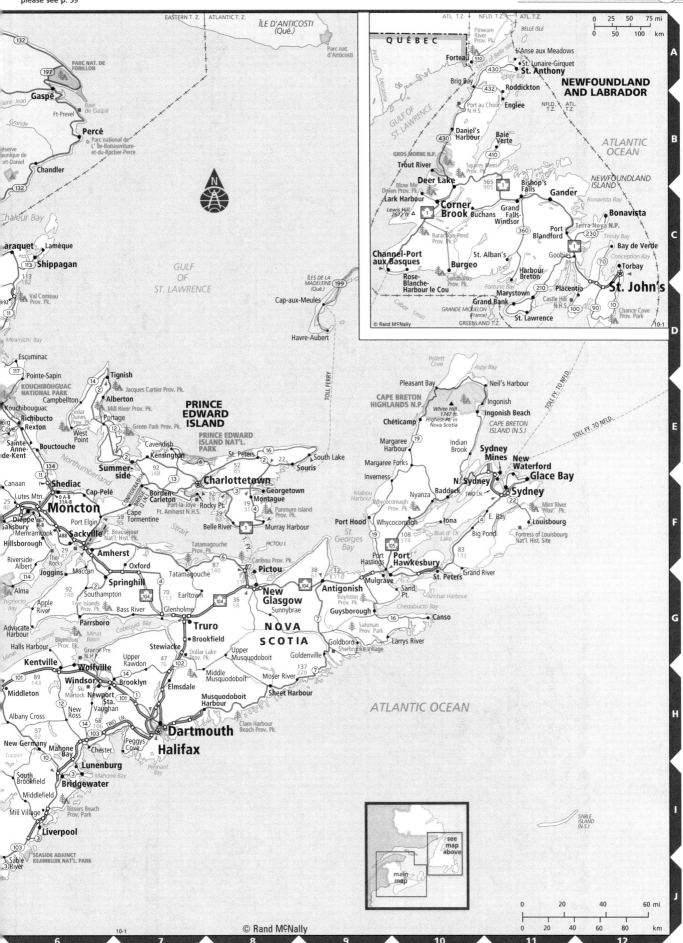

ÎLE D'ANTICOSTI
(Qué.)

Parc nat.
d'Anticosti

EASTERN T. Z.   ATLANTIC T. Z.   ATL. T.Z.   NFLD. T.Z.   ATL. T.Z.

QUÉBEC

0   25   50   75 mi
0   50   100 km

Forteau
Pinware
River
Prov. Pk.

BELLE ISLE

Strait of Belle Isle
L'Anse aux Meadows
St. Lunaire-Girquet
St. Anthony

**NEWFOUNDLAND
AND LABRADOR**

Brig Bay
Roddickton

Port au Choix
N.H.S.
Englee

NFLD.   ATL.
T.Z.   T.Z.

GULF
OF
ST. LAWRENCE

Daniel's
Harbour
Baie
Verte

*ATLANTIC
OCEAN*

*NEWFOUNDLAND
ISLAND*

Gaspé

Ft-Prevel

Baie
de Gaspé

Percé

Parc national de
L'Île-Bonaventure-
et-du-Rocher-Percé

Chaleur Bay

Chandler

Réserve
faunique de
Port-Daniel

PARC NAT. DE
FORILLON

Saint-Jean

Grande

GROS MORNE N.P.

Trout River

Squires Mem.
Prov. Pk.

Blow Me
Down Prov. Pk.
Deer Lake

565
905

Bishop's
Falls

Gander

Lark Harbour

Lewis Hill
2672 ft

**Corner
Brook** Buchans

Grand
Falls-
Windsor

Bonavista Bay

Bonavista

Terra Nova N.P.

Port
Blandford

Baraachois Pond
Prov. Pk.

Lamèque

Shippagan

araquet

113
182

113

Val Comeau
Prov. Pk.

GULF
OF
ST. LAWRENCE

ÎLES DE LA
MADELEINE (Qué.)

199

Cap-aux-Meules

Havre-Aubert

360

St. Alban's

**Channel-Port
aux Basques**

Burgeo

Rose-
Blanche-
Harbour le Cou

Sandbanks
Prov. Pk.

Harbour
Breton

Marystown

Fortune Bay

Grand Bank

GRANDE MIQUELON
(France)

210
St. Lawrence

Placentia

Castle Hill
N.H.S.

100

Goobies

210

Chance Cove
Prov. Park

70

Conception Bay

Torbay

St. John's

90

10

Bay de Verde

Trinity Bay

© Rand McNally

GREENLAND T.Z.

10-1

Miramichi Bay

Escuminac

Pointe-Sapin

117

KOUCHIBOUGUAC
NATIONAL PARK

Campbellton

Kouchibouguac

Richibucto

Big
Cove

Rexton

Sainte-
Anne-
de-Kent

Bouctouche

Canaan

134

Northumberland

11

Shediac
Cap-Pelé

0 A-B
11A-B

Moncton

Lutes Mtn.
25
40

Dieppe
Salisbury
Memramcook

467
A-B

Port Elgin

59
7

Cape
Tormentine

Sackville

488

Ft. Beauséjour
Nat'l. Hist. Site

Hillsborough

Riverside-
Albert

114

Amherst

The
Rocks

29
47

Joggins

Maccan

Oxford

Springhill

92
148

4

Southampton

Five Islands
Prov. Pk.

Bass River

Earltown

Alma

Tignish

14   2

Jacques Cartier Prov. Pk.

Alberton

Mill River Prov. Pk.

Cedar
Dunes
Prov. Pk.

Portage

**West
Point**

12

Green Park Prov. Pk.

**PRINCE
EDWARD
ISLAND**

PRINCE EDWARD
ISLAND NAT'L.
PARK

Cavendish

Kensington

2

**Summer-
side**

92
148

13

Borden-
Carleton

Port-la-Joye-
Ft. Amherst N.H.S.

CONFEDERATION
BRIDGE (2 LN.)

Charlottetown

6

St. Peters

16

22

Souris

South Lake

52
85

Cape
Traverse

3

19
31

Rocky Pt.

Montague

52
63

Panmure Island
Prov. Pk.

Georgetown

Belle River

1

Murray Harbour

CONFEDERATION BRIDGE

PICTOU I.

6

Caribou Prov. Pk.

7

87
140

Pictou

38
61

32
51

Tatamagouche
Prov. Pk.

Strait

Cape

Tatamagouche

**New
Glasgow**

Sunnybrae

Antigonish

Boylston
Prov. Pk.

Sand
Pt.

Aichat Harbour

70
113

104

104

36
58

Truro

Brookfield

**NOVA
SCOTIA**

7

Guysborough

16

Chedabucto Bay

Canso

Glenholme

Cobequid Bay

Parrsboro

**Advocate
Harbour**

Chignecto
Bay

Apple
River

Blomidon
Prov. Pk.

Halls Harbour

Minas

Minas
Basin

Grange Pre
N.H.P.

Stewiacke

Dollar Lake
Prov. Pk.

Upper
Musquodoboit

Goldboro

Salsman
Prov. Park

Larrys River

Sherbrooke Village

Kentville

Wolfville

101

89
143

Windsor

Ski
Martock

Upper
Rawdon

47
76

102

Middle
Musquodoboit

Goldenville

137
220

7

Middleton

12

Newport
Sta.

1

New
Vaughan

Elmsdale

**Musquodoboit
Harbour**

Moser River

Albany Cross

New
Ross

66
106

57
92

TWO LN.

103

Dartmouth

Halifax

Clam Harbour
Beach Prov. Pk.

Sheet Harbour

ATLANTIC OCEAN

New Germany

Mahone
Bay

Tupper

10

Chester

Peggys
Cove

Lunenburg

Pennant
Bay

Mahone Bay

South
Brookfield

Bridgewater

Middlefield

Mill Village

103

Liverpool

103

SEASIDE ADJUNCT
KEJIMKUJIK NAT'L. PARK

Sable
River

3

Rissers Beach
Prov. Park

Pollett
Cove

Aspy Bay

Pleasant Bay

Neil's Harbour

**CAPE BRETON
HIGHLANDS N.P.**

Ingonish

White Hill
1747 ft
Highest Pt. in
Nova Scotia

Ingonish Beach

Chéticamp

CAPE BRETON
ISLAND (N.S.)

TOLL FY. TO NFLD.

TOLL FY. TO NFLD.

Margaree
Harbour

19

Indian
Brook

Margaree Forks

Inverness

Mabou
Harbour

Nyanza

Baddeck

TWO LN.

**Sydney
Mines**

N. Sydney

**New
Waterford**

Glace Bay

Sydney

22

Mira River
Prov. Pk.

Whycocomagh
Prov. Pk.

Iona

Louisbourg

Port Hood

19

Whycocomagh

St.
Georges
Bay

108
174

Bras D'Or
Lake

E. Bay

Big Pond

Fortress of Louisbourg
Nat'l. Hist. Site

Port
Hastings

**Port
Hawkesbury**

105

83
133

St. Peters

Grand River

Mulgrave

SABLE
ISLAND
(N.S.)

see
map
above

main
map

0   20   40   60 mi
0   20   40   60   80   km

© Rand McNally

10-1

6   7   8   9   10   11   12

For border crossing information, please see p. 59

Mexico

Population: 103,263,388
Land area: 758,450 sq. mi.
Capital: Mexico City

Cities and Towns

Mexico City

Ciudad de México (Mexico City)

Puerto Rico (U.S.)

© Rand McNally

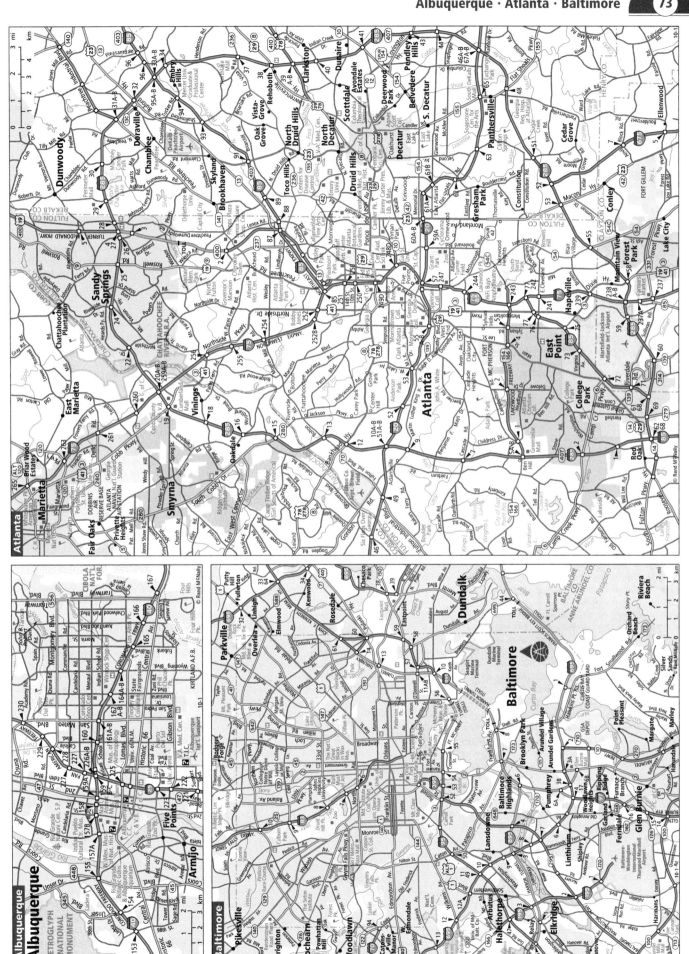

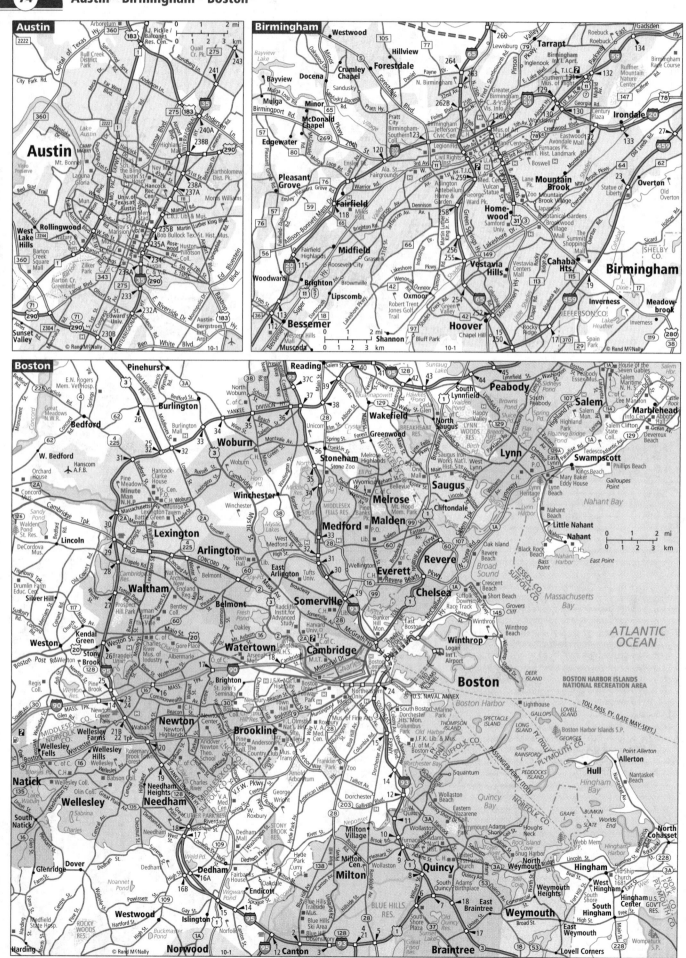

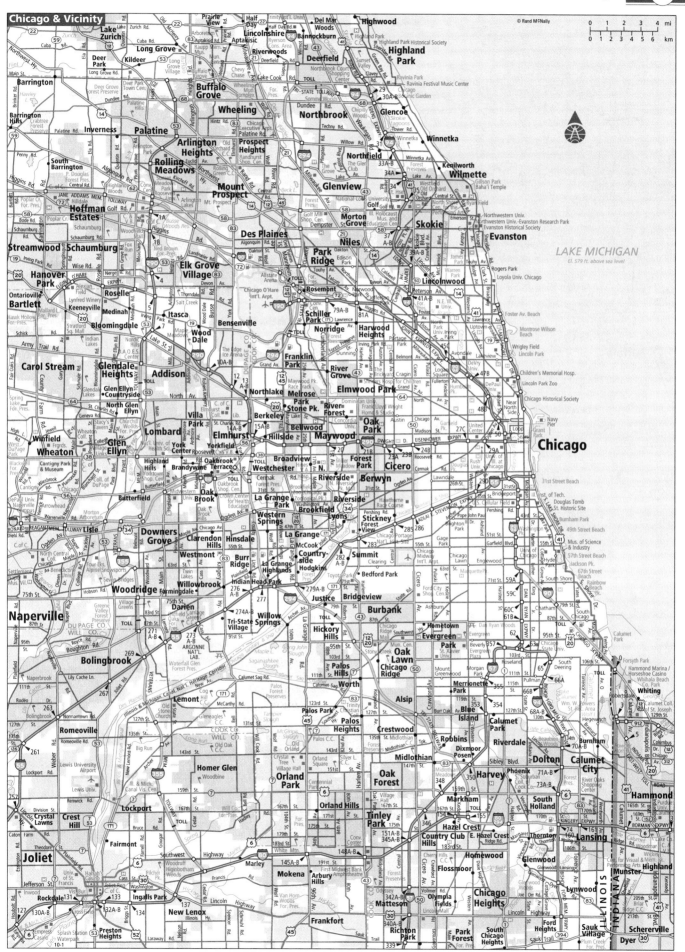

Chicago & Vicinity

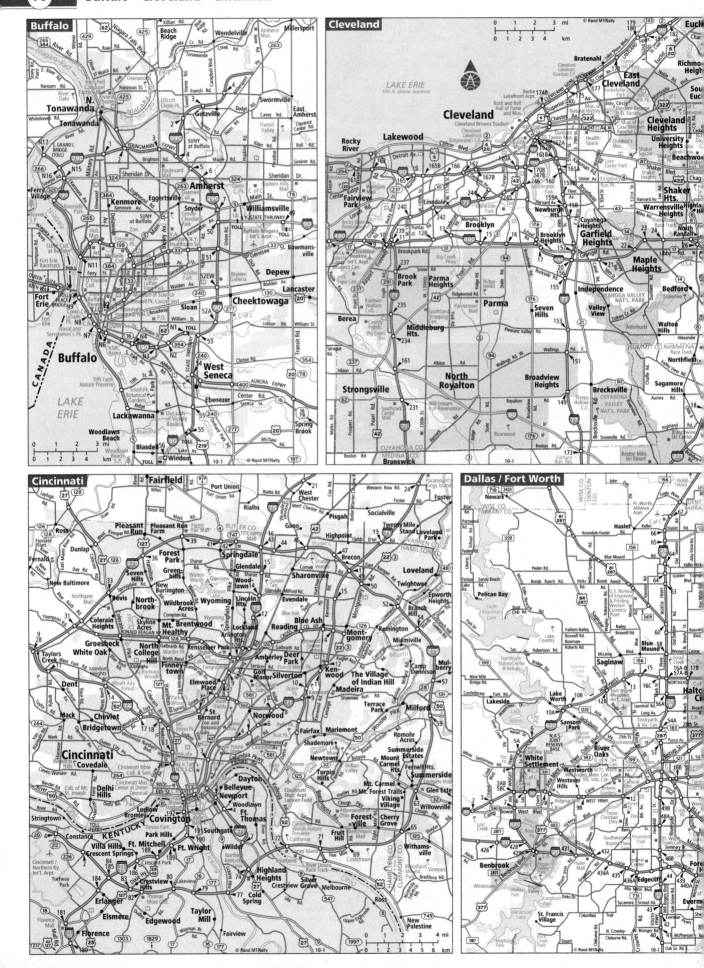

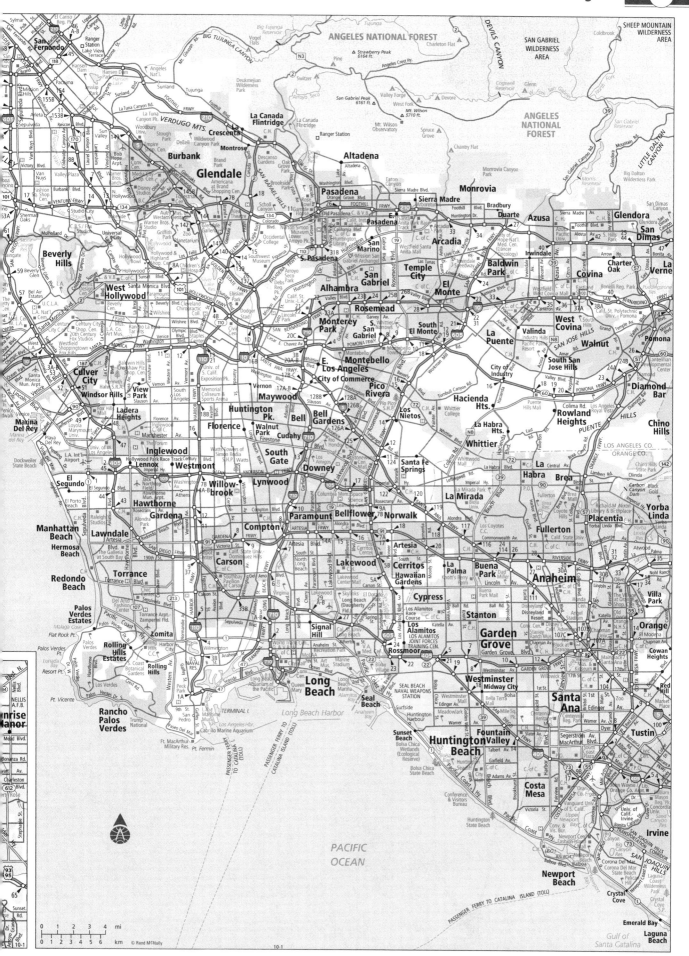

PACIFIC
OCEAN

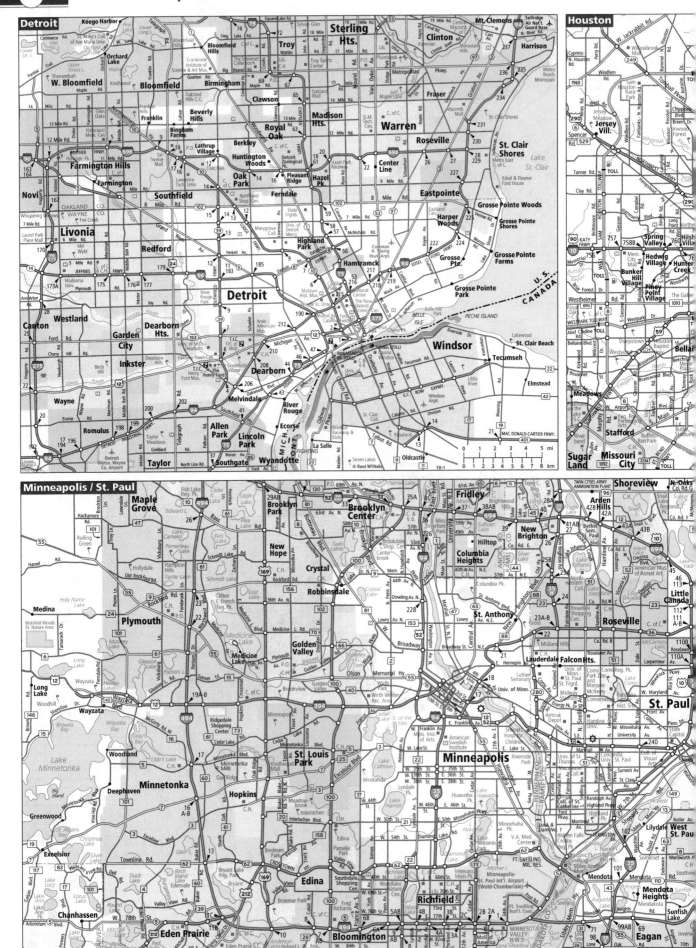

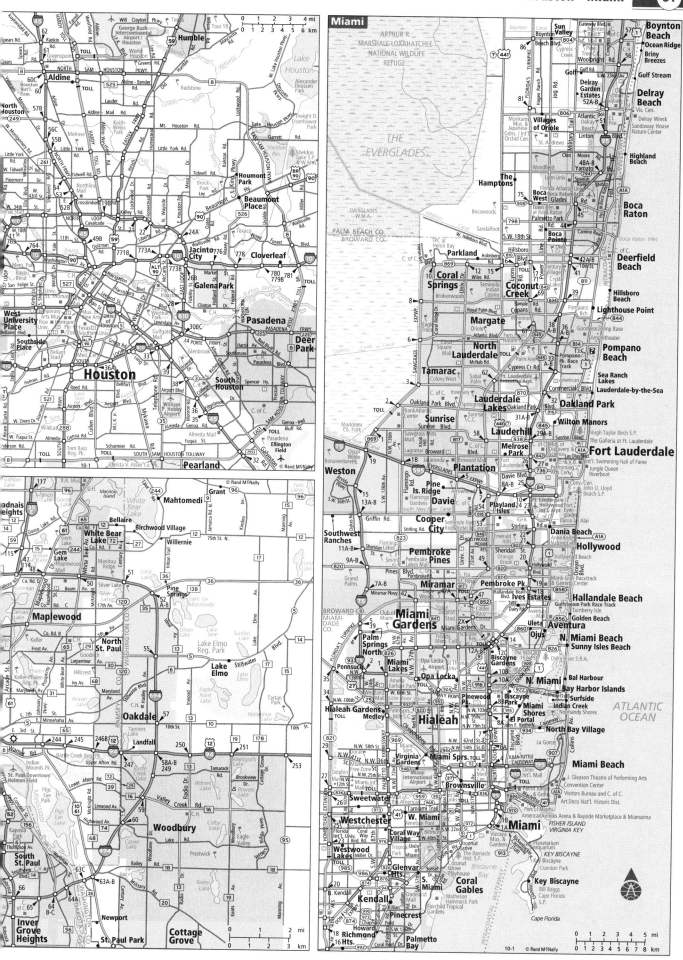

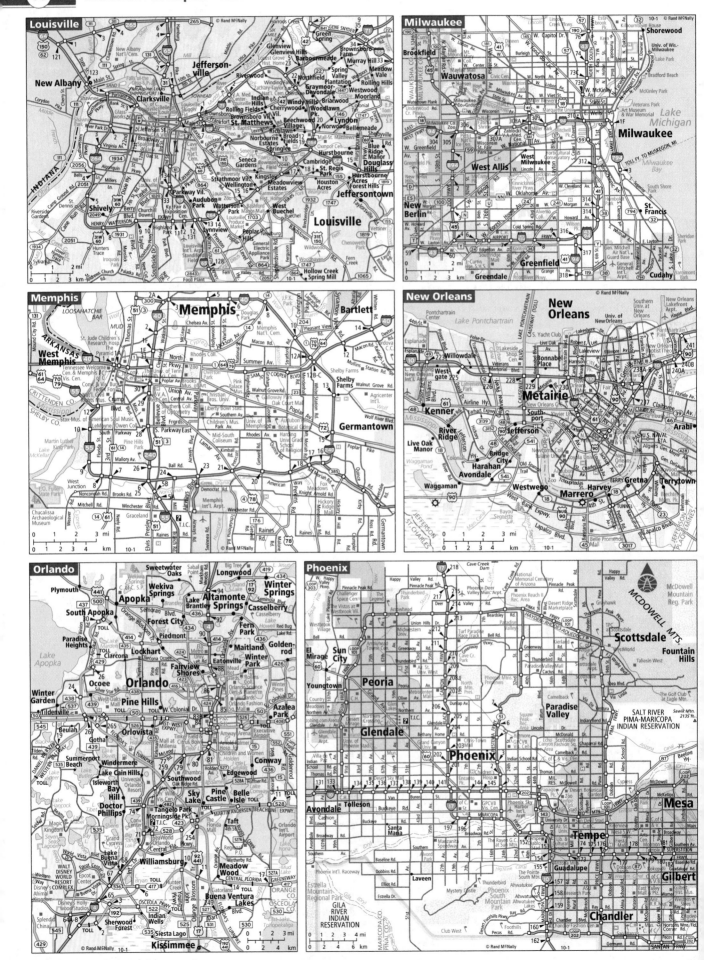

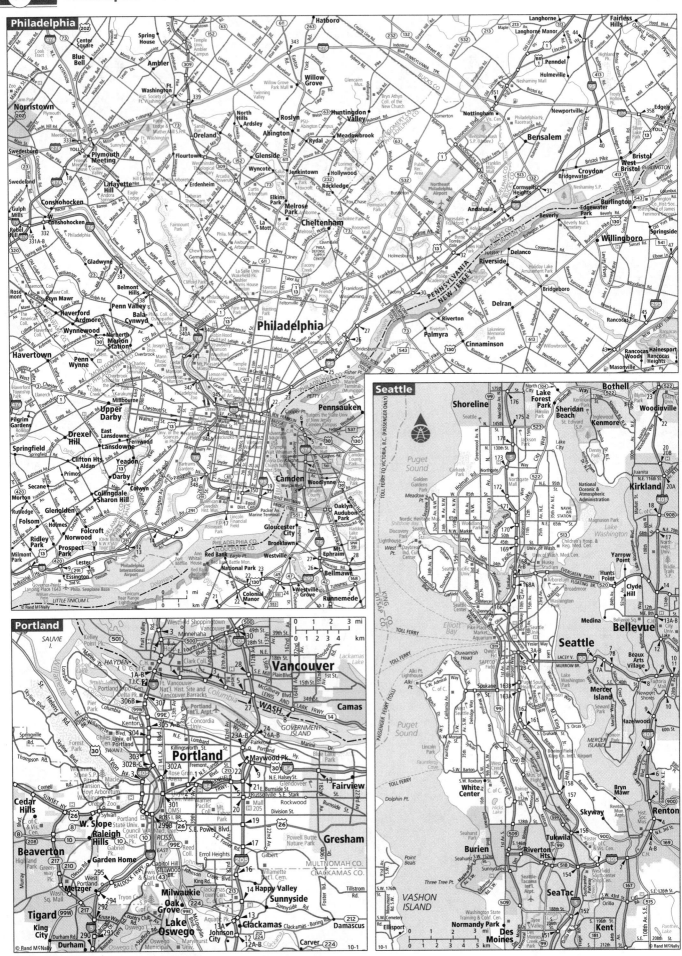

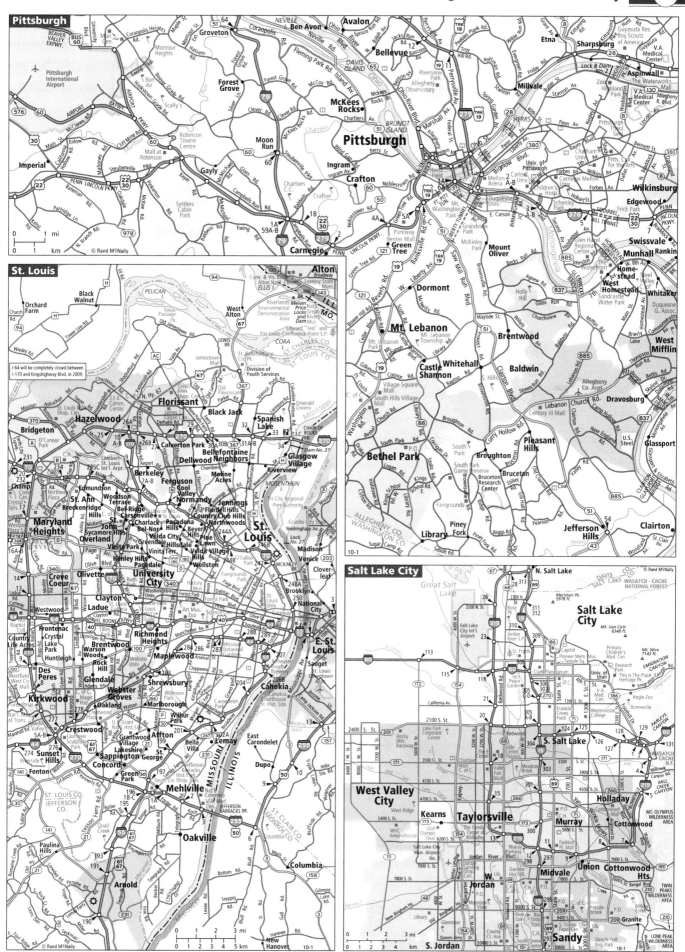

Pittsburgh

St. Louis

I-64 will be completely closed between I-170 and Kingshighway Blvd. in 2009.

Salt Lake City

© Rand McNally

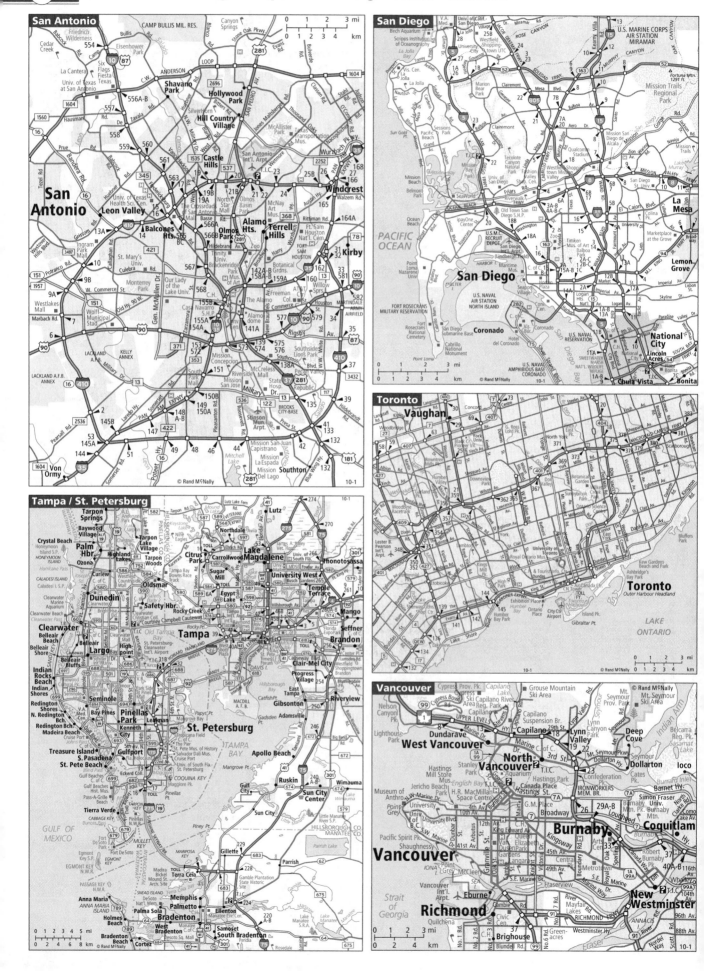

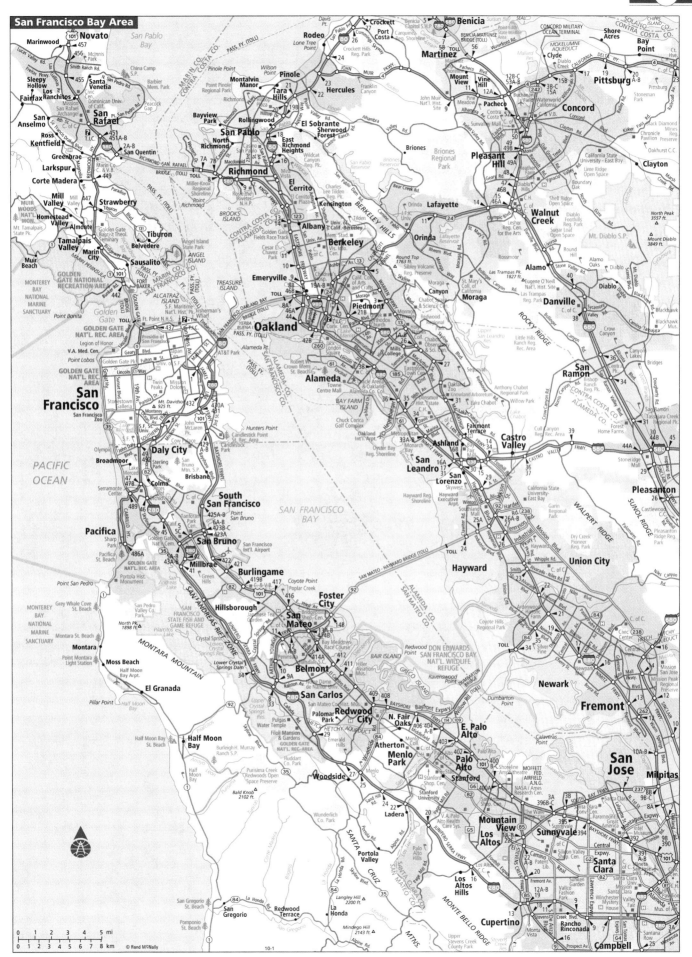

San Francisco Bay Area

PACIFIC OCEAN

SAN FRANCISCO BAY

San Francisco

Oakland

San Jose

Fremont

Hayward

Pleasanton

San Ramon

Danville

Walnut Creek

Concord

Pittsburg

Martinez

Benicia

Richmond

Berkeley

San Rafael

Novato

Pacifica

Half Moon Bay

Redwood City

Palo Alto

Mountain View

Sunnyvale

Santa Clara

Milpitas

Cupertino

Campbell

MONTEREY BAY NATIONAL MARINE SANCTUARY

GOLDEN GATE NATIONAL RECREATION AREA

0 1 2 3 4 5 mi
0 1 2 3 4 5 6 7 8 km

© Rand McNally

10-1

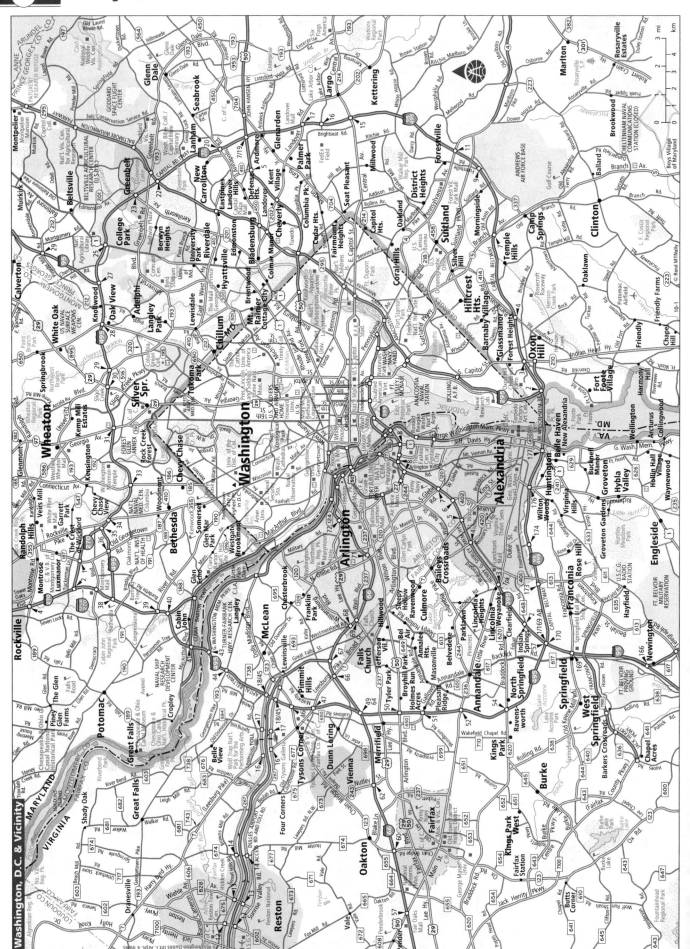

TOURISM CONTACTS

On the road or before you go, log on to the official tourism website of your destination. These websites offer terrific ideas about organizing a visit and often include calendars of special events and activities. Prefer calling? Most states offer toll-free numbers.

Alabama Bureau of Tourism & Travel
(800) 252-2262
(334) 242-4169
www.800alabama.com

Alaska Travel Industry Association
(907) 929-2200
www.travelalaska.com

Arizona Office of Tourism
(866) 275-5816
www.arizonaguide.com

Arkansas Department of Parks & Tourism
(800) 628-8725
www.arkansas.com

California Travel & Tourism Commission
(800) 862-2543*
(916) 444-4429
www.visitcalifornia.com

Colorado Tourism Office
(800) 265-6723
www.colorado.com

Connecticut Tourism
(888) 288-4748
www.ctvisit.com

Delaware Tourism Office
(866) 284-7483
www.visitdelaware.com

Visit Florida
(888) 735-2872
(850) 488-5607
www.visitflorida.com

Georgia On My Mind
(Georgia Department of Economic Development)
(800) 847-4842
www.georgiaonmymind.org

Hawaii Visitors & Convention Bureau
(800) 464-2924
www.gohawaii.com

Idaho Division of Tourism Development
(800) 847-4843
(208) 334-2470
www.visitidaho.org

Illinois Bureau of Tourism
(800) 226-6632
www.enjoyillinois.com

Indiana Office of Tourism Development
(800) 677-9800
www.visitindiana.com

Iowa Tourism Office
(800) 345-4692*
(888) 472-6035
(515) 242-4705
www.traveliowa.com

Kansas Department of Commerce, Travel & Tourism
(800) 252-6727
www.travelks.com

Kentucky Department of Travel
(800) 225-8747
www.kentuckytourism.com

Louisiana Office of Tourism
(800) 334-8626
www.louisianatravel.com

Maine Office of Tourism
(888) 624-6345
www.visitmaine.com

Maryland Office of Tourism
(866) 639-3526
www.visitmaryland.org

Massachusetts Office of Travel & Tourism
(800) 227-6277
(617) 973-8500
www.massvacation.com

Travel Michigan
(800) 644-2489
www.michigan.org

Explore Minnesota Tourism
(888) 868-7476
(651) 296-5029
www.exploreminnesota.com

Mississippi Division of Tourism
(800) 927-6378
(866) 733-6477
www.visitmississippi.org

Missouri Division of Tourism
(800) 519-2100
(573) 751-4133
www.visitmo.com

Travel Montana
(800) 847-4868
www.visitmt.com

Nebraska Division of Travel & Tourism
(877) 632-7275
(800) 228-4307
www.visitnebraska.org

Nevada Commission on Tourism
(800) 638-2328
(775) 687-4322
www.travelnevada.com

New Hampshire Division of Travel and Tourism Development
(800) 386-4664
www.visitnh.gov

New Jersey Division of Travel & Tourism
(800) 847-4865
www.visitnj.org

New Mexico Tourism Department
(800) 733-6396
www.newmexico.org

New York State Division of Tourism
(800) 225-5697
www.iloveny.com

North Carolina Division of Tourism
(800) 847-4862
(919) 733-8372
www.visitnc.com

North Dakota Tourism Division
(800) 435-5663
www.ndtourism.com

Ohio Division of Travel & Tourism
(800) 282-5393
www.discoverohio.com

Oklahoma Tourism & Recreation Department
(800) 652-6552
www.travelok.com

Travel Oregon
(800) 547-7842
www.traveloregon.com

Pennsylvania Tourism Office
(800) 847-4872
www.visitpa.com

Rhode Island Tourism Division
(888) 886-9463*
(800) 556-2484*
(800) 250-7384
www.visitrhodeisland.com

South Carolina Department of Parks, Recreation & Tourism
(888) 727-6453*
(803) 734-1700
www.discoversouthcarolina.com

South Dakota Office of Tourism
(800) 732-5682
www.travelsd.com

Tennessee Department of Tourist Development
(800) 462-8366*
(615) 741-2159
www.tnvacation.com

Texas Tourism
(800) 888-8839*
www.traveltex.com

Utah Office of Tourism
(800) 200-1160
(801) 538-1030
www.utah.com

Vermont Department of Tourism and Marketing
(800) 837-6668
www.vermontvacation.com

Virginia Tourism Corporation
(800) 847-4882
www.virginia.org

Washington State Tourism
(800) 544-1800
www.experiencewashington.com

Destination DC
(800) 422-8644
(202) 789-7000
www.washington.org

West Virginia Division of Tourism
(800) 225-5982
(304) 558-2200
www.wvtourism.com

Wisconsin Department of Tourism
(800) 432-8747
(608) 266-2161
www.travelwisconsin.com

Wyoming Travel & Tourism
(800) 225-5996
(307) 777-7777
www.wyomingtourism.org

Canada

Travel Alberta
(800) 252-3782
www.travelalberta.com

Tourism British Columbia
(800) 435-5622
www.hellobc.com

Travel Manitoba
(800) 665-0040
(204) 927-7800
www.travelmanitoba.com

Tourism New Brunswick
(800) 561-0123
www.tourismnewbrunswick.ca

Newfoundland & Labrador Tourism
(800) 563-6353
(709) 729-2830
www.newfoundlandlabrador.com

Nova Scotia Department of Tourism, Culture & Heritage
(800) 565-0000
(902) 425-5781
novascotia.com

Ontario Travel
(800) 668-2746
www.ontariotravel.net

Tourism Prince Edward Island
(800) 463-4734
www.gentleisland.com

Tourisme Québec
(877) 266-5687
(514) 873-2015
www.bonjourquebec.com

Tourism Saskatchewan
(877) 237-2273
www.sasktourism.com

Mexico

Mexico Tourism Board
(800) 446-3942
www.visitmexico.com

*To request travel materials only

MILE MARKERS — MILEAGE CHART

This handy chart offers more than 2,400 mileages covering 77 North American cities. Want more mileages? Visit go.randmcnally.com/MC and type in any two cities or addresses.

Mileages in this chart are based upon the routes usually followed by motorists. Highway systems include interstate, U.S., and state highways.

City	Albuquerque, NM	Atlanta, GA	Billings, MT	Boston, MA	Charlotte, NC	Chicago, IL	Cincinnati, OH	Dallas, TX	Denver, CO	Detroit, MI	Houston, TX	Indianapolis, IN	Kansas City, MO	Los Angeles, CA	Memphis, TN	Miami, FL	Milwaukee, WI	Minneapolis, MN	New Orleans, LA	New York, NY	Omaha, NE	Orlando, FL	Philadelphia, PA	Phoenix, AZ	Pittsburgh, PA	Portland, OR	Saint Louis, MO	Salt Lake City, UT	San Francisco, CA	Seattle, WA	Washington, DC	Wichita, KS
Albuquerque, NM		1386	998	2219	1626	1333	1387	647	446	1570	884	1279	784	786	1008	1952	1354	1225	1165	2001	863	1730	1924	462	1641	1363	1037	599	1086	1438	1885	591
Amarillo, TX	284	1102	965	1935	1342	1049	1103	363	424	1286	589	995	570	1072	720	1668	1132	1009	881	1716	647	1446	1640	746	1357	1669	752	883	1370	1743	1600	382
Atlanta, GA	1386		1831	1095	244	715	461	780	1444	722	794	533	800	2174	379	661	809	1127	468	882	992	440	780	1844	684	2603	555	1878	2472	2649	637	955
Atlantic City, NJ	1985	831	2072	338	590	818	632	1518	1792	644	1598	703	1187	2774	1063	1248	910	1232	1273	126	1272	1038	60	2447	365	2922	948	2201	2934	2889	188	1379
Austin, TX	705	920	1495	1959	1164	1121	1128	193	950	1358	157	1067	702	1381	643	1341	1204	1136	503	1737	839	1124	1658	1010	1411	2068	825	1304	1760	2143	1524	542
Baltimore, MD	1887	683	1953	400	442	699	513	1368	1673	524	1448	584	1068	2670	914	1082	792	1112	1124	192	1153	889	98	2349	246	2804	829	2081	2816	2771	39	1260
Billings, MT	998	1831		2236	1946	1246	1546	1425	551	1535	1652	1435	1026	1240	1477	2497	1173	838	1868	2041	845	2275	2011	1210	1713	891	1278	552	1173	818	1951	1064
Birmingham, AL	1241	146	1780	1177	390	660	466	636	1329	724	668	478	749	2030	235	746	754	1072	343	960	939	534	880	1700	748	2551	502	1826	2327	2598	745	810
Boise, ID	938	2177	621	2660	2336	1693	1943	1702	830	1960	1930	1835	1372	842	1825	2844	1732	1461	2216	2465	1225	2622	2435	914	2137	428	1622	339	639	503	2375	1338
Boston, MA	2219	1095	2236		841	983	870	1764	1970	724	1844	937	1421	2983	1312	1482	1074	1396	1520	207	1436	1288	306	2681	570	3086	1182	2365	3098	3054	439	1613
Branson, MO	864	652	1241	1433	868	545	601	435	806	784	602	493	209	1651	274	1284	630	643	597	1201	402	1062	1138	1326	851	2013	249	1288	1950	2060	1081	292
Calgary, AB	1542	2357	541	2615	2400	1627	1925	1967	1096	1916	2209	1814	1567	1557	2028	3018	1555	1221	2419	2439	1287	2797	2391	1524	2093	787	1820	869	1500	678	2334	1606
Charleston, SC	1703	317	2133	970	207	908	620	1099	1706	826	1105	726	1103	2491	696	583	1002	1324	742	768	1294	380	668	2165	634	2904	857	2180	2789	2951	532	1272
Charlotte, NC	1626	244	1990	841		769	477	1023	1566	616	1038	583	961	2414	619	728	867	1180	712	641	1151	526	539	2088	446	2761	714	2037	2712	2808	398	1092
Chicago, IL	1333	715	1246	983	769		289	926	1002	280	1085	181	526	2015	531	1381	90	408	923	787	470	1153	757	1795	459	2118	296	1398	2130	2063	697	724
Cincinnati, OH	1387	461	1546	870	477	289		934	1187	259	1055	108	584	2172	482	1127	381	703	804	637	722	905	571	1849	288	2369	348	1647	2380	2363	512	779
Cleveland, OH	1598	714	1597	638	514	342	248	1194	1330	168	1315	315	799	2342	729	1240	436	756	1057	460	1043	428	2060	131	2446	560	1725	2458	2414	370	992
Columbus, OH	1457	567	1606	763	426	354	106	1039	1261	191	1174	176	657	2244	587	1164	445	766	910	533	792	954	468	1920	184	2439	421	1718	2451	2425	411	851
Corpus Christi, TX	855	1001	1622	2051	1244	1338	1262	410	1077	1542	207	1228	919	1494	782	1394	1421	1353	554	1844	1056	1172	1754	1122	1561	2218	1042	1454	1873	2292	1619	758
Dallas, TX	647	780	1425	1764	1023	926	934		880	1163	228	873	489	1437	453	1307	1010	928	519	1548	656	1086	1467	1066	1221	2128	630	1403	1734	2193	1332	361
Denver, CO	446	1404	551	1970	1566	1002	1187	880		1270	1035	1083	603	1015	1097	2069	1042	913	1398	1775	534	1851	1732	908	1447	1256	854	533	1268	1320	1671	519
Des Moines, IA	983	902	946	1299	1057	332	580	683	670	599	938	474	193	1682	617	1567	372	242	1008	1165	131	1339	1074	1445	777	1786	354	1015	1764	1015	391
Detroit, MI	1570	722	1535	724	616	280	259	1163	1270		1319	288	764	2281	742	1354	374	696	1066	613	736	1144	583	2032	285	2385	533	1664	2397	2353	522	964
Duluth, MN	1375	1187	860	1370	1239	466	760	1092	1063	754	1331	651	586	2076	963	1852	394	152	1354	1264	530	1632	1230	1838	932	1749	679	1458	2033	1677	1171	785
Edmonton, AB	1724	2391	722	2549	2443	1670	1968	2149	1278	1958	2391	1857	1626	1755	2147	3058	1598	1264	2538	2482	1445	2836	2434	1721	2136	966	1878	1069	1695	793	2377	1787
El Paso, TX	260	1418	1257	2373	1662	1455	1569	635	707	1702	744	1398	929	796	1089	1934	1497	1377	1095	2202	1004	1712	2102	424	1774	1630	1157	866	1175	1705	1967	730
Fargo, ND	1318	1361	607	1629	1414	641	937	1079	873	930	1321	825	600	1848	1054	2025	569	235	1445	1438	420	1807	1405	1593	1107	1487	710	1781	1424	1348	1645	1099
Gatlinburg, TN	1439	196	1803	922	202	578	290	884	1376	552	964	396	773	2226	431	865	672	994	640	707	964	640	625	1901	493	2574	527	1850	2525	2621	490	905
Guadalajara, JA	1194	1739	2194	2789	1982	1954	1962	1028	1639	2191	948	1901	1535	1501	1482	2131	2037	1969	1292	2592	1672	1910	2492	1212	2261	2545	1658	1792	1963	2631	2356	1377
Gulfport, MS	1221	399	1912	1482	643	896	767	562	1386	1025	403	780	883	1949	365	792	988	1196	78	1266	1073	572	1180	1577	1052	2633	647	1909	2307	2730	1036	867
Houston, TX	884	794	1652	1844	1038	1085	1055	228	1035	1319		1021	732	1550	575	1186	1163	1171	347	1633	954	1154	2356	784	1634	1929	2431	1411	595
Indianapolis, IN	1279	533	1435	937	583	181	108	873	1083	288	1021		482	2068	464	1198	272	591	818	707	613	968	643	1742	359	2260	243	1541	2273	2253	582	674
Jacksonville, FL	1636	346	2183	1146	379	1068	796	992	1756	1002	871	874	1152	2421	677	349	1163	1474	547	939	1344	141	844	2050	825	2954	907	2230	2723	3001	706	1272
Kansas City, MO	784	800	1026	1421	961	526	584	489	603	764	732	482		1616	451	1466	565	436	844	1196	187	1246	1127	1246	840	1797	250	1073	1808	1844	1066	193
Key West, FL	2099	809	2646	1659	886	1534	1275	1445	2222	1515	1334	1348	1611	2884	1159	162	1632	1944	1010	1446	1807	387	1357	2514	1332	3417	1370	2693	3186	3464	1213	1735
Las Vegas, NV	572	1959	973	2714	2199	1746	1932	1220	747	2013	1457	1828	1349	270	1581	2525	1786	1656	1739	2518	1273	2803	2480	286	2190	1023	1609	419	569	1128	2428	1164
Lexington, KY	1371	369	1610	917	400	370	83	876	1186	344	996	184	581	2158	423	1030	464	782	745	701	771	817	638	1833	370	2381	334	1657	2392	2428	533	773
Little Rock, AR	877	515	1407	1447	754	650	617	319	965	885	439	583	381	1666	137	1147	724	815	425	1230	574	925	1150	1340	905	2211	345	1488	1963	2275	1015	446
Los Angeles, CA	786	2174	1240	2983	2414	2015	2172	1437	1015	2281	1550	2068	1616		1794	2735	2055	1925	1894	2787	1546	2515	2713	370	2428	963	1821	688	380	1134	2670	1377
Memphis, TN	1008	379	1477	1312	619	531	482	453	1097	742	575	464	451	1794		1012	622	831	394	1094	641	778	1014	1471	768	2245	283	1524	2095	2299	879	577
Mexico City, DF	1404	1718	2301	2768	1962	2017	1979	1090	1756	2254	924	1963	1598	1839	1500	2111	2100	2032	1272	2571	1735	1889	2471	1469	2279	2768	1721	2043	2336	1440
Miami, FL	1952	661	2497	1482	728	1381	1127	1307	2069	1354	1186	1198	1466	2735	1012		1475	1791	861	1288	1658	229	1180	2362	1173	3260	1221	2544	3038	3315	1044	1587
Milwaukee, WI	1354	809	1173	1074	867	90	381	1010	1042	374	1163	272	565	2055	622	1475		336	1015	879	509	1258	849	1817	551	2062	379	1437	2170	1990	788	763
Minneapolis, MN	1225	1127	838	1396	1180	408	703	928	913	696	1171	591	436	1925	831	1791	336		1223	1204	372	1573	1171	1687	874	1727	563	1308	2040	1655	1110	634
Mobile, AL	1234	328	1874	1427	571	917	721	589	1414	978	468	733	850	2014	382	719	1011	1224	144	1202	1038	497	1101	1643	1000	2661	645	1936	2320	2727	965	894
Montréal, QC	2129	1218	2099	310	980	847	824	1722	1832	560	1884	847	1330	2845	1314	1647	938	1262	1640	382	1302	1437	454	2591	603	2948	1092	2228	2960	2916	587	1529
Nashville, TN	1219	248	1586	1099	407	469	273	664	1158	534	786	287	555	2006	212	913	564	881	532	884	747	692	802	1682	560	2357	310	1633	2306	2404	667	688
New Orleans, LA	1165	468	1868	1520	712	923	804	519	1398	1066	347	818	844	1894	394	861	1015	1223		1304	1032	641	1222	1523	1090	2642	675	1920	2252	2716	1087	880
New York, NY	2001	882	2041	207	641	787	637	1548	1775	613	1632	707	1094	2788	879	1204	1304	1245	1089		97	2463	369	2891	954	2170	2902	2858	228	1391
Norfolk, VA	1910	558	2132	569	328	878	605	1350	1758	704	1362	720	1155	2707	898	950	969	1295	1026	370	1335	755	271	2373	425	2962	911	2238	2973	2949	189	1349
Oklahoma City, OK	542	844	1203	1678	1084	792	846	204	631	1029	437	739	348	1326	466	1476	876	788	722	1460	452	1254	1384	1005	1101	1922	496	1200	1627	1948	1344	158
Omaha, NE	863	992	845	1436	1151	470	722	656	534	736	898	613	187	1546	641	1658	509	372	1032	1245		1436	1212	1325	914	1650	439	930	1662	1663	1151	298
Orlando, FL	1730	440	2275	1288	526	1153	905	1086	1851	1144	965	968	1246	2515	778	229	1258	1573	641	1089	1436		986	2145	975	3048	999	2323	2816	3093	849	1365
Ottawa, ON	2039	1158	1768	428	920	760	732	1632	1748	471	1804	757	1240	2763	1230	1618	895	1032	1582	440	1553	1408	447	2501	546	2660	1002	2142	2877	2586	566	1439
Philadelphia, PA	1924	780	2011	306	539	757	571	1467	1732	583	1547	643	1127	2713	1014	1180	849	1171	1222	97	1212	986		2387	304	2873	888	2140	2873	2828	137	1319
Phoenix, AZ	462	1844	1210	2681	2088	1795	1849	1066	908	2032	1178	1742	1246	370	1471	2362	1817	1687	1523	2463	1325	2145	2387		2104	1332	1499	653	749	1414	2348	1053
Pittsburgh, PA	1641	684	1713	570	446	459	288	1221	1447	285	1354	359	840	2428	768	1173	551	874	1090	369	914	975	304	2104		2563	604	1842	2574	2530	244	1035
Portland, ME	2315	1192	2333	110	938	1079	967	1861	2067	825	1940	1034	1518	3082	1408	1585	1176	1492	1616	304	1533	1385	402	2778	666	3186	1279	2461	3196	3151	535	1710
Portland, OR	1363	2603	891	3086	2761	2118	2369	2128	1256	2356	2260	1727	1963	2245	3260	2062	1727	2642	2891	1950	3048	2861	1332	2563		2050	765	835	172	2800	1764
Rapid City, SD	843	1508	323	1900	1670	912	1208	1061	397	1200	1291	1100	704	1312	1160	2173	840	575	1551	1708	525	1956	1675	1305	1378	1251	959	649	1384	1142	1618	699
Reno, NV	1019	2396	958	2881	2555	1913	2163	1668	1051	2180	1904	2056	1591	470	2029	3063	1953	1818	2186	2685	1445	2841	2656	733	2357	578	1844	518	217	720	2595	1558
Richmond, VA	1832	532	2051	547	293	797	512	1278	1671	622	1329	627	1069	2620	824	944	888	1210	1002	334	1259	742	245	2294	344	2869	822	2145	2880	2868	108	1261
Saint Louis, MO	1037	555	1278	1182	714	296	348	630	854	531	783	243	281	1221	283	1221	379	563	675	954	439	999	888	1449	604	2050		1326	2061	2096	827	442
Salt Lake City, UT	599	1878	552	2365	2037	1398	1647	1403	533	1664	1634	1541	1073	688	1524	2544	1437	1308	1920	2170	930	2323	2140	653	1842	765	1326		735	839	2079	1042
San Antonio, TX	712	986	1480	2039	1230	1202	1210	276	935	1439	197	1149	766	1357	727	1379	1285	1205	541	1822	920	1160	1742	985	1495	2076	906	1311	1736	2150	1607	625
San Diego, CA	810	2138	1302	3046	2381	2080	2196	1359	1077	2346	1472	2089	1597	120	1819	2656	2118	1986	1816	2809	1613	2436	2738	352	2452	1083	1845	750	501	1256	2693	1401
San Francisco, CA	1086	2472	1173	3098	2712	2130	2380	1734	1268	2397	1929	2273	1808	380	2095	3038	2170	2040	2252	2902	1662	2816	2873	749	2574	635	2061	735		807	2812	1775
Santa Fe, NM	58	1379	943	2212	1618	1313	1379	640	391	1562	877	1272	766	840	998	1944	1336	1207	1158	1994	891	1723	1917	520	1634	1388	1029	625	1154	1463	1879	572
Sault Ste. Marie, ON	1777	1040	1273	923	947	471	577	1370	1428	347	1527	540	951	2465	972	1685	398	538	1355	921	850	1475	911	2240	614	2166	740	1848	2581	2090	854	1150
Seattle, WA	1438	2649	818	3054	2808	2063	2363	2193	1320	2353	2431	2253	1844	1134	2299	3315	1990	1655	2716	2858	1663	3093	2828	1414	2530	172	2096	839	807		2768	1828
Spokane, WA	1320	2369	541	2774	2528	1785	2084	1964	1091	2075	2192	1973	1564	1216	2018	3035	1712	1377	2409	2580	1383	2814	2550	1381	2252	351	1817	720	874	278	2490	1600
Tampa, FL	1746	451	2293	1342	578	1166	916	1102	1860	1178	980	984	1222	2525	779	255	1260	1578	651	1138	1445	84	1040	2153	1023	3064	1008	2340	2832	3111	904	1381
Toronto, ON	1800	963	1771	548	756	519	493	1393	1504	232	1551	518	1001	2517	983	1483	609	933	1306	489	1784	1497	2262	316	2620	763	1899	2632	2588	486	1188
Tulsa, OK	645	782	1234	1576	1022	687	738	258	692	927	487	635	243	1433	402	1414	773	704	671	1350	380	1192	1282	1107	994	1938	392	1215	1731	2012	1234	173
Vancouver, BC	1575	2785	953	3188	2944	2198	2499	2338	1465	2487	2565	2389	1980	1275	2437	3451	2125	1790	2851	2993	1799	3229	2963	1550	2665	313	2232	973	947	141	2903	1973
Washington, DC	1885	637	1951	439	398	697	512	1332	1671	522	1411	582	1066	2670	879	1044	788	1110	1087	228	1151	849	137	2348	244	2800	827	2079	2812	2768		1258
Wichita, KS	591	955	1064	1613	1092	724	779	361	519	964	595	674	193	1377	577	1587	763	634	880	1391	298	1365	1319	1053	1035	1764	442	1042	1775	1828	1258	